The Future of
Intelligence

To the men and women of the intelligence services of the Western democracies, who perform extraordinary and crucial service within the law and under difficult conditions.

The Future of Intelligence

Mark M. Lowenthal

polity

First published in 2018 by Polity Press

Reprinted 2019

Polity Press
65 Bridge Street
Cambridge CB2 1UR, UK

Polity Press
101 Station Landing, Suite 300
Medford, MA 02155 USA

ISBN-13: 978-1-5095-2028-2 (hardback)
ISBN-13: 978-1-5095-2029-9 (paperback)

A catalogue record for this book is available from the British Library.

Typeset in 11 on 13 pt Sabon
by Toppan Best-set Premedia Limited
Printed and bound in the United States by LSC Communications

Library of Congress Cataloging-in-Publication Data

Names: Lowenthal, Mark M., author.
Title: The future of intelligence / Mark M. Lowenthal.
Description: Cambridge, UK ; Malden, MA : Polity, 2017. | Includes
    bibliographical references and index.
Identifiers: LCCN 2017009316 (print) | LCCN 2017038694 (ebook) | ISBN
    9781509520312 (Mobi) | ISBN 9781509520329 (Epub) | ISBN 9781509520282
    (hardback) | ISBN 9781509520299 (paperback)
Subjects: LCSH: Intelligence service--United States--Planning. | Intelligence
    service--United States--Forecasting. | BISAC: POLITICAL SCIENCE /
    Political Freedom & Security /Intelligence.
Classification: LCC J K468.I6 (ebook) | LCC J K468.I6 L644 2017 (print) | DDC
    327.1273--dc23
LC record available at https://lccn.loc.gov/2017009316

Contents

Preface

In Greek mythology, the ability to see the future came at a high price. Prometheus, whose name means "foresight," gave fire to man and was condemned to eternal painful punishment by Zeus. Teiresias, the seer in the Oedipus cycle, received foresight from Zeus to compensate for being blinded by Hera. Cassandra, a princess of Troy, may be most pertinent for an intelligence officer. Apollo gave her the gift of prophecy but, when she spurned him, he condemned Cassandra never to be believed.

I trust that writing a book on the future of intelligence is less fraught with danger. But it is, nonetheless, difficult. Intelligence is, at once, easy to define but amorphous. There are three essential activities in intelligence: collecting intelligence; analyzing intelligence; and conducting certain operations. Within each category are a variety of types of collection, analysis, and operations. Everything else is supportive of these three core functions. Each of these activities has a long past and both good and not-so-good traditions. In addition, each of them is conducted differently in every country, even among nations whose intelligence services are closely allied, such as the United States and Britain.

Why write this book now? The answer is that intelligence has gone through and will continue to go through a series of changes brought about by both technology and events, all done in the midst of increased scrutiny and public knowledge. Intelligence professionals may see this as a potentially dangerous combination, and that may be so, but they are also manageable if handled properly in the early phases. That said, this book is not intended to be prescriptive. It is more like reconnaissance, surveying the surrounding terrain to ascertain its features and to determine where the opposition may lie. In this case, the terrain is intelligence itself as well as the factors, issues, and trends that will both challenge intelligence and require it to change.

Throughout the long history of the Cold War there was something remote about intelligence. Even though the ultimate threat was a strategic nuclear exchange between the West and the Soviet Union this seemed, except for a few very specific crises, a far-off possibility. The Soviet menace was real enough but it did not seem overly proximate to the average citizen, unless you were close to the edge of the Iron Curtain itself. The terrorist war that is usually dated from September 11, 2001 – although al Qaeda attacks date back to at least 1992 – has been marked by attacks on the homeland in the United States, London, Madrid, and later, Paris and Nice. This was more troubling and created immediate and understandable political demands for intelligence "to do something" about it. This sort of shortsighted sentiment is always dangerous for intelligence officers, because policy makers and the public want action, and most do not care about the specifics, until they learn about them later or have time to reflect. This certainly has been the case for US intelligence, which found itself deserted by many of those same Members of Congress who had urged it to any and all action in the days immediately after 9/11.

As noted, this intelligence activity also took place within a greatly changed information milieu: the twenty-four-hour news cycle, which is often a beast that must be fed, especially when there is not much news; and the rise of social media of all sorts, which requires no authentication, and tends to be dominated by people seeking reinforcement of their views rather than probing them for veracity. To this we must add the effect of intelligence leaks, especially that perpetrated by Edward Snowden, a contract employee of the National Security Agency, which not only exposed the details of legally enacted collection programs but much else besides that had nothing to do with the programs that Snowden said had prompted his actions. But the public discourse following these leaks was dominated by those expressing outrage. Little time or space was given to those who understood the legality and the necessity of the programs.

I have framed the discussion in this book as a series of vectors or choices that offer both opportunities and potential obstacles or threats to intelligence, depending on how they are addressed. As I said, I have tried to be a scout, not a seer. I see this book as part of an important ongoing conversation about how and where intelligence could be headed in the years ahead.

Several words of thanks are in order. First, to the staff of Polity Press, especially Louise Knight, who invited me to undertake this task, and Nekane Tanaka Galdos, who oversaw the process. Several individuals were very generous with their time and expertise, offering important insights from which I have greatly profited: first and foremost, my wife Cynthia; also Jamie Baker, Christopher Bidwell, Robert Clark, Dewey Houck, Letitia Long, Carmen Medina, William Nolte, Harvey Rishikof, Lewis Shepherd, Douglas Thomas, and Alan Wade. Cynthia also read and edited the entire manuscript, greatly improving both the argumentation and the flow. I must also mention our children, Sarah and Adam, for their constant support and encouragement.

I also had the opportunity to speak with US and foreign intelligence officials who were very generous with their time but will remain anonymous.

None of the above-named individuals is responsible for the views or opinions expressed in this book.

1
What this Book is About

Intelligence – initially defined here somewhat narrowly as the effort to obtain and to analyze information required by national leaders – has a long past. Intelligence is one of the oldest organized human activities, often referred to somewhat archly as "the second oldest profession." The recorded reigns of rulers and the chronicles of their wars are older. But the oldest reference to intelligence in Western literature is the story in the *Book of Numbers*, about the spies sent into Canaan by Moses shortly after the Hebrews' exodus from Egypt. Believed to have been written in the sixth century BCE, *Numbers* describes events that occurred perhaps some 900 to 1000 years before. In the east, Sun Tzu, whose life is believed to be roughly contemporaneous with the compilation of *Numbers*, drew on many centuries of Chinese military experience when he wrote *The Art of War*, which includes much useful advice on the importance of intelligence. It is striking that these two civilizations – the Jews and the Chinese – thousands of miles apart and with no likely knowledge of one another, should both describe the use of intelligence in fairly contemporaneous periods.

Intelligence has a long past. What sort of future does it have? There is irony here, as intelligence is supposed to be about the future – although more on that later – and yet most intelligence analysts understand how difficult it is to achieve this future vision with any clarity. Two twentieth-century icons – Nobel physicist Niels Bohr and American baseball player Yogi Berra – are both credited with observing that: "It is very difficult to make predictions, especially about the future."

And, so, here I am trying to prognosticate about the future of a profession whose function is to prognosticate about the future. This can appear to be either rather circular or self-absorbed.

My goal is not to predict specific outcomes for the future of intelligence or even which international security issues will be paramount, neither of which is possible. Policy makers and intelligence officers can forecast some specific events with a certain degree of accuracy but foretelling major trends – either in policy or in intelligence – is much more difficult. For example, it was self-evident that several Arab state leaders – Hosni Mubarak in Egypt, Zine El Abidine Ben Ali in Tunisia – were old and nearing the end of their tenures. However, the outbreak of the much more widespread Arab Spring protests after the self-immolation of a Tunisian fruit seller could not have been foreseen.

Determining ongoing intelligence requirements is sometimes confused with forecasting the next series of events that will need to be addressed. These are different activities. Properly done, an intelligence requirements system should be a reflection of the current priorities of the policy makers, the people whom intelligence serves and supports. This was the view we had in mind when I led the effort to implement the National Intelligence Priorities Framework (NIPF) in 2003, and then managed for its first two years. Our goal in creating the NIPF, and the continuing goal fourteen years after its adoption, is to get a firm understanding of the ongoing priorities of the President and his senior national security appointees and advisers in terms of both the issues on which to focus and the relative rank importance to be given to each. However, as I always warned my staff as we managed the NIPF, we had to expect that issues would arise that had either originally been given a low priority and were now deemed more important, or were not given any priority at all. This is the reality of conducting intelligence: you have your list of issues and the world has its own. This very necessary requirements activity is far different from forecasting the next important event in international politics.

Also, a realistic intelligence priorities system, will, of necessity, focus on current or near-term issues. These issues are uppermost in policy makers' minds and agendas. Few policy makers have the time to focus for prolonged periods on issues that seem far off or even possibilities as opposed to likely certainties. When I managed the NIPF we actually tried to create what we called a "shadow NIPF," looking ahead two or three years. This was not a success. Most analysts said their issue would look "pretty much" as it did now. Again, this was understandable, as it is difficult to foresee major unsettling change. To quote Yogi Berra again: "The future will be like the past, only different."

Intelligence, like all other human endeavors, has both revolutionary and evolutionary aspects. There are issues that arise and seem significant, only to turn out to be ephemeral, just as there are issues that seem small in importance and turn out to be very important. Sorting these out as they occur is difficult enough. Forecasting them in the future is even more daunting.

With those cautionary observations made, what is it we are talking about when we talk about intelligence?

At a somewhat abstract but basic level, we are talking about the ability to determine needs for certain types or categories of information that are not readily available to us, the ability to collect that information and then to analyze and put it into some form or format so that the person who needs the now-assessed intelligence can access it and consider it. More concretely, we are talking about the ability of the state to conduct these collection and analytic activities, as well as to carry out certain operations that are different from both diplomacy and military operations.

At this level, prognostication is relatively simple. Policy makers will always have a need for information that is not readily available. The types of information will vary – depending on current circumstances and issues and the preferences of the policy makers – but the core need for intelligence will continue. That said, intelligence appears to have reached a turning point. The convergence of several factors and issues – rapidly changing technology, greater public availability of information, increased streams of information from certain sources, more threatening transnational issues, and changing tolerance among governments and people for what types of intelligence collection and operations should be conducted in their names – all pose challenges for the future of intelligence. Many of these factors can be either positive or negative, depending on how they develop or how policy makers and intelligence officers react to them. These issues form the core of this book. But the essential view here is that intelligence is a normal state function conducted at various levels by different governments, and that it will continue to exist, albeit with possibly changed means and perhaps ends.

Another framing note: this book focuses primarily on the future of intelligence in democratic states. Within that group of states, much of this book will also be written from the perspective of the United States. Of all the democracies, the United States has the largest and most capable intelligence establishment. It therefore tends to serve as a leader by sheer dint of size and capability. We further assume that most – if not all – democracies, largely follow the procedural intelligence model of the United States, Britain, et al.: intelligence works for and is subordinated to policy but intelligence has no meaningful existence beyond that relationship. For the Five Eyes partners (US, UK, Australia, Canada, and New Zealand) this also means that intelligence officers do not make policy recommendations. That is the exclusive sphere of elected officials and their appointees in the policy departments. These rules are crucial assumptions for assessing the future of intelligence because if they were no longer in force then any further prognostications would be fanciful at best and more likely meaningless. In other words, intelligence works best when confined to its proper sphere and relationship to policy.

Intelligence is a difficult function to conduct under any form of government, although the constraints are very different under authoritarian versus democratic governments. Authoritarian governments by definition exhibit different degrees of control and repression over their population. Parts of their intelligence apparatus will serve some of these domestic policing functions in addition to their foreign ones. In many authoritarian countries a key attribute is that their security service serves both an internal and external function. This was the case for the Soviet Union, and now for China, and may again be the case for Russia as Vladimir Putin reassembles the KGB, which was largely an internal service with one directorate that was assigned foreign intelligence responsibilities. This leads to an interesting conundrum for these intelligence services. The authoritarian intelligence service does not want dissent to get out of hand. Therefore, true dissent or political disinterest may be under-reported to avoid having the intelligence services appear incompetent. The KGB apparently had no real insight into the degree of public disinterest in the future of the Soviet state per se as the Soviet Union came to an end. At the same time, the authoritarian intelligence service cannot claim to have totally stifled dissent lest the government question why the service is still required or still required at that level of activity or why some level of dissent is still evident despite these claims. In other words, a low level of dissent – real or imagined – is most useful for both the authoritarian rulers – hence the need for their extensive powers – and for their intelligence services.

Another constraint for intelligence in authoritarian states is the likely limit on being able to report "bad news," or intelligence that conflicts with the official line. This runs counter to one of the basic premises of most authoritarian states, the superior wisdom of the rulers, which justifies their continuation in power. Indeed, running an intelligence service in an authoritarian state is risky at a personal level. The intelligence leadership can too easily be seen as a possible threat or rival by the political leaders. The intelligence officers know too many intimate secrets. Of the four heads of Soviet intelligence under Josef Stalin, only one, Vyacheslav Menzhinsky, died of natural causes. Similarly, Chinese President Xi Jinping's anti-corruption drive against "tigers and flies" (meaning both high- and low-ranking officials), has convicted several senior intelligence officials, including Zhou Yongkang, a former Minister of Public Security.

This is not to suggest that policy makers in democracies never have the urge to "shoot the messenger" – at least metaphorically if not bureaucratically. They do, but the risks are professional and political but not personal. In democracies all senior positions are inherently political. Of the twenty-one individuals who have been US Directors of Central Intelligence or Directors of National Intelligence, six were fired by Presidents (Dulles, Helms, Colby, Deutch, Goss, Blair); three lost their jobs as a result of a partisan change in control of the Presidency (Bush, Turner, Gates); and two quit in frustration over their lack of access to the President (McCone, Woolsey).

The constraints for intelligence services in democracy are quite different. The concepts of civil liberties and the rule of law place immediate bounds on what intelligence can or cannot do. Various types of intelligence collection against either domestic or foreign targets require authorization from elected officials or their confirmed designees or from various types of legal overseers. Funding invariably comes from elected legislatures, which gives the legislatures both insights and degrees of control as well. Courts are available for redress if individuals believe intelligence services have contravened their charters. The concept of secrecy, upon which all intelligence services rely regardless of the government they serve, conflicts with the democratic concept of open governments.

But the point remains that intelligence in democracies is substantially different from intelligence in authoritarian states and the focus in this book is on intelligence as practiced in democracies. Some of the issues discussed, particularly in technology, are more generic in nature. But many of the other issues, particularly the conduct of and possible limits on collection and operations and the broader issue of governance are very different and more meaningful in democratic states. Even here one can find fairly broad variance: Israel tolerates operational intelligence activities that the United States does not; Canada tolerates very few at all. Still, the fundamental concept of governments subject to the rule of law and to popular will are broad enough to allow some level of generalization.

Why write this book now? Intelligence agencies in democracies have not previously operated with the degrees of both publicity and scrutiny that are now expected and actually experienced on a recurring basis. Several factors account for this change.

The first factor has been the great increase in the role of legislative oversight of intelligence, primarily in the United States but in Britain, Australia, and France as well. In the United States this change was driven by the unraveling of the Cold War consensus because of the Vietnam War, which ended in 1975, and then by a series of leaks and revelations about US intelligence activities in 1974–6. One of the conclusions of the revelations and the subsequent investigations by a commission headed by Vice President Nelson Rockefeller and then by Senate and House select committees, was that congressional oversight had been both trusting and lax. Both chambers then created permanent committees dedicated specifically to intelligence oversight. The investigations also changed how journalists viewed intelligence, going from a topic about which little was said and little written to one that was seen as fair game for revelations.

The previous period of gentlemanly journalistic respect for secrecy was now over. Intelligence has never been able to retreat to its former largely undiscussed status.

The second and more important, more recent factor has been the effect of the ongoing war against terrorists or, rather, their war against us. Terrorists' ability to reach into various nations to carry out attacks – either directly or through self-avowed supporters – has increased the public's concern about the quality of their respective intelligence services. In the mid-1990s, I was the staff director of the House Permanent Select Committee on Intelligence. The chairman, Larry Combest, a Republican from Texas, said to me early in our relationship: "Do you know what the American people want from intelligence? They want to know that when they go to bed at night they will wake up in the same country in the morning." If Combest's formulation is correct, then we lost that sense of security on the morning of September 11, 2001. By mid-morning, we were in a different country – or, as L. P. Hartley wrote in *The Go-Between* (1953): "The past is a foreign country: they do things differently there." There was a substantial difference between the pre- and post-September 11 United States.

The long Cold War struggle with the Soviet Union and periods after 1945 when we have had forces actively engaged in combat all required good intelligence support but were at the same time somewhat remote form the everyday lives of citizens. The advent of terror attacks on the homeland, as we now call it, changed that. Intelligence was not just a foreign policy issue; it became a public safety issue.

An investigation into what went wrong on September 11 was inevitable. In fact, there were two investigations, one by the Joint Inquiry of the House and Senate Intelligence Committees, and then one by the 9/11 Commission (formally, the National Commission on Terrorist Attacks Upon the United States). (By contrast, there were eight investigations of the Pearl Harbor attack between 1941 and 1946.) The goal of the 9/11 Commission staff from the outset was to reorganize US intelligence. The unstated premise of the Commission was that there had to have been some way that the 9/11 attack could have been prevented. This was an understandable desire, as to believe otherwise is to accept the fact of a rather discomforting vulnerability. The commission found various flaws in policy and intelligence but they never found the one or two or more things that, had they been done correctly, would have led to the intelligence necessary to stop those four airplanes on that September morning.

Hard on the heels of the 9/11 attack and its aftermath came the national intelligence estimate (NIE) on weapons of mass destruction (WMD) in Iraq. British and Australian intelligence also produced assessments on this issue. Three important points need to be made about the Iraq WMD NIE. First, yes, the estimate was largely (not entirely) incorrect. Second, as the Senate Select Committee on Intelligence's investigation stated, the NIE was not politicized; that is, it was not written expressly to support President George W. Bush's decision to go to war. Indeed, the estimate was written at the request of the Senate, not the Bush administration. Third, despite the fact that it was largely wrong, the NIE was not influential in the US decision to go to war. As noted, the Bush administration did not request the estimate, although they had been assured that the Intelligence Community assessed that there were WMD in Iraq. The NIE had no effect on the Senate vote (77–23 authorizing the use of force against Iraq) as only six Senators actually read the estimate and several more were briefed on the contents by staff, leaving a large majority who voted to go to war but never delved into the intelligence at all. Finally, the UN Security Council also rejected Secretary of State Colin Powell's briefing based on the NIE and refused to support the United States and Britain's use of force.

However, the fact of an erroneous estimate coming so soon after the 9/11 attacks raised significant questions about US intelligence capabilities.

Then there have been the strains created by the role of intelligence in the war against terrorists: the rendition (extra-judicial arrests) and prolonged detention of terrorists, the use of enhanced interrogation techniques, and the use of armed drones across a fairly wide geographic range have all focused more attention on and raised new questions about the role and future of intelligence.

There have also been the effects of a cascade of leaks, primarily provided by Edward Snowden, that have raised further questions about the conduct of intelligence and about the level of public support now required to conduct intelligence.

Concerns have also been raised about the relationship between the new Trump administration and US intelligence. The first issue was Trump's very harsh reactions to reports that Russia had made attempts to interfere in the 2016 US election in support of Trump. The second was an initial restructuring on National Security Council (NSC) membership, which limited the attendance of the Director of National Intelligence and the Chairman of the Joint Chiefs of Staff to a "by invitation" basis. Past practice had been for both officials to attend NSC and NSC Principals' Committee meetings as the intelligence and military advisers. Several observers believed that this boded ill for the overall level of expertise at NSC meetings and especially for the role and value placed upon intelligence. Subsequently, these changes were rescinded.

Finally, the international system appears to be going through a period of great flux or uncertainty. Although transnational issues like terrorism, WMD proliferation and climate change are important, these all occur within a system of nation states. As DNI James Clapper has noted: "Intelligence is not about things and it is not about places. It is about things in places." In other words, one must be able to connect issues with places or actors – meaning either nation states or non-state actors, or determine which issues matter in a given place. Given the premise that intelligence is a normal function of most states then the nature of nation states in the future is also an important determinant in the future of intelligence.

Nation states have been the predominant international actors since the Peace of Westphalia in 1648, which ended the Thirty Years War in Europe. Besides settling a series of religious and territorial questions, Westphalia created the international system we have known ever since, a system of sovereign states, supposedly free from outside interference in their domestic affairs. Regardless of the form of government – monarchy, republic, authoritarian of various types – the nation state has been the essential actor and unit of account in international affairs.

One of the striking aspects of the mid- to late-twentieth century was how stable this system was in terms of both general peace and in terms of the boundaries of states. The general peace, after a century marked by two World Wars, is usually attributed to the Cold War and the advent of nuclear weapons, which put a premium on settling major disputes between the two main antagonists before they led to armed conflict. As for state boundaries, which are one of the ultimate definitions of any state, a view appeared to have arisen after World War II that state borders were now sacrosanct and not subject to further change. One of the few practical and useful measures taken by the Office of African Unity (OAU 1963–2002) was the decision to accept the artificial boundaries drawn by the European colonial powers in Africa. But beginning in the late twentieth century, this boundary shibboleth began to break down, first in what had been Yugoslavia, then in the USSR and then in the Middle East (Iraq, Syria) after the Second Gulf War. More recently, we have seen Russia's disregard of boundaries when it annexed the Crimea from Ukraine in 2014.

To be sure, the states listed above were all multi-national states whose internal cohesion was problematic at best. But there have been strong indications of regional discontent within states that appeared to be more cohesive – Scotland in the United Kingdom and the Basque region of Spain. Thus, at least in the near term, state cohesion may not be what it was. Second, the essential condition of state sovereignty, control over one's borders, has also broken down, particularly in the Middle East and then in Europe. The refugees' desire to live some place free from war and terror has breached European nations' control of their borders, both on the exterior of Europe and then within the passport-free Schengen Zone. Also, the rise of more vocal immigrant rights groups in Europe, the United States, and Australia would appear to suggest that immigrants or their advocates believe that immigrants have the right to live wherever they want, regardless of the preferences of the state. So, to some extent, a key concept of state sovereignty has either broken down or is being questioned.

This is not to suggest that nation-state actors will disappear or be less important. They will not. But some of their hallmarks will change. The two key hallmarks that will not change are the desire on the part of all states for stability and for as much economic well-being as is possible, in part for its own sake and in part for the political stability that this affords.

The Cold War ended in 1991 with the demise of the Soviet Union. We then entered a rather amorphous period of international relations that was somewhat backwards looking, often called the post-Cold War world. Although the terrorist attack of 9/11 became one of the most striking events of that period, it is now fifteen years since 9/11. The war against terrorists continues but it is less dominant as an issue than it was. The rise of China and the revanchism of Russia are at once new issues and also familiar ones, reminiscent of the old nation-state issues that once dominated the national security agenda.

There may be no more cohesive or orderly international arrangement than what we have now, which makes the creation and prosecution of policy more difficult and should insure the ongoing utility, if not importance, of intelligence. The status quo has never been wholly stable, even during the Cold War. One of the primary roles of intelligence is to identify these sources of instability as subjects for either warning or opportunity, as we will discuss later.

The key function that intelligence plays for policy makers, aside from the essential strategic warning function, is decision advantage, a concept first defined by Jennifer Sims, a professional intelligence officer and scholar in the academic intelligence field. Policy makers have goals, things they want to achieve, as well as things they wish to avoid or prevent. But states exist in a system that exhibits a great deal of friction, to borrow a term from Clausewitz, meaning all the things that impede one's ability to achieve one's goals. One of the main sources of friction is other states, who have goals of their own. Decision advantage means providing policy makers with the intelligence they need to have an advantage in pursuing their goals and in dealing with rival states.

One of the main decision advantages of intelligence, as I have written elsewhere, is the ability of intelligence to reduce policy makers' uncertainty. Wise policy makers know that they cannot know the outcomes of all of the decisions they make; they may not even be certain, at times, of which issues to address first. Good intelligence will address this uncertainty by attempting to describe which outcomes or reactions are more or less likely and therefore where to focus one's attention. The goal is to circumscribe the uncertainty, not eliminate it. Given the typical schedule of a senior policy official, having some guide as to where to spend the most time is no small advantage, nor is being prepared for certain outcomes more than others. Of course, there is always the possibility that the intelligence may be wrong but that is one of the perils of being an intelligence officer.

Providing decision advantage and circumscribing uncertainty are both fundamental functions of intelligence *vis-à-vis* policy makers that are unlikely to change.

One major issue for intelligence in the future will be to keep track of, and ahead of, the levers of power. States have various perceived levers of power: size, location, military strength, resources, economics, demographics. But these levers change over time, and some levers that were once seen as important prove to be less meaningful in the future. For example, nuclear weapons meant a great deal to the United States and the Soviet Union in terms of their bilateral relationship but proved to be meaningless when either power had to deal with guerrilla wars, the United States in Vietnam and the Soviet Union in Afghanistan. Natural resources, even crucial ones, can wax and wane in importance. After the Arab oil embargo imposed during the October 1973 war in the Middle East it was widely assumed that oil would provide the producing states with significant wealth and leverage from that point on. Predictions abounded about the very finite amount of oil available in the future. All of this proved to be false. First, the oil-producing nations could not agree on production quotas and so undercut one another in price while refusing to adhere to production quotas. Second, new technologies, such as fracking, created an overabundance of oil, driving prices down to the point where many nations too dependent on oil for income have suffered: Russia, Iran, Venezuela, and others. Even Saudi Arabia has had to float loans and consider selling a stake in Aramco, its oil company.

What are the levers that are likely to matter in the future, and who has them, will be a constant focus for intelligence. Capabilities in information technology, often broadly referred to as cyber, may confer advantages but also introduce a number of vulnerabilities. Will these net out as an advantage or disadvantage in the future?

This book is about the ability of government intelligence services to provide intelligence support – both analysis and operations – in the future, how this service may change and why, and where there may be competitors to these services.

The book addresses these prospective changes in three categories:

- Changes in technology, including intelligence collection,

- The role of analysis, and
- Issues of governance.

Each of these areas is comprised of a series of vectors that can go in more than one possible direction when it comes to the future of intelligence. Like any good intelligence officer, my goal is not to forecast exactly what will happen in these areas but to pose a series of outcomes, positive and negative, that seem more or less likely. In some cases there may be more questions about the future direction of intelligence than there are answers. But this should not be a problem. At this point knowing the questions may be more of a service than suggesting answers that will be more susceptible to error. Raising the right questions is a good starting point for a debate in a democracy.

2
Technology Vectors

An introductory word of caution about this chapter: several of my close colleagues who may be reading this now are undoubtedly aghast at the idea – if not the hubris – of my writing anything about technology. I have a well-earned reputation as a "late adopter" of most technologies, seen as a skeptic, and sometimes accused of being a Luddite. To be clear, I am not a Luddite; I would not advocate a halt to technological advances. But I am a skeptic, which is not unusual for an intelligence analyst overall, and that may not be a bad stance to take as one sifts through much of the hype that surrounds new and burgeoning technology, and attempts to get at the core of what these very varied technologies may mean for intelligence.

Technology is inherently neutral, neither good nor bad. What matters is the use to which the technology is being put. An internal combustion engine can power an ambulance or a tank. Nuclear science can produce medical isotopes or nuclear weapons. This observation about the inherent neutrality of technology extends to several of the current areas of technological concern for intelligence.

Technology is of interest to intelligence agencies for three primary reasons:

(1) The technology enables current or new capabilities or creates new opportunities;
(2) The technology poses a new or changed threat;
(3) The technology arises in a field wholly unrelated to intelligence but fits into one or both of the above categories. The rise of social media would be a good example of this.

It is important to keep in mind that a technology may fit any and all of these categories at any given time. The key for intelligence is to keep abreast of both the threats and opportunities.

This chapter discusses technology in two veins: emerging technologies that offer both positive and negative vectors for how intelligence agencies do business; and technology with regard to the collection of intelligence.

One of the major advantages and dependencies of US intelligence in the twentieth and twenty-first centuries has been technology. For example, the development of computer technology is intimately connected with twentieth-century intelligence, beginning with the World War II code-breaking efforts at Bletchley Park: the two British-built machines used against German codes, the electro-mechanical Bombe, and Colossus, the first electronic, digital, programmable computer. Today's super-computers owe their existence to the intelligence community.

Beginning with the U-2 aircraft in 1955, and then moving to intelligence collection satellites in 1961, the United States has derived tremendous advantage from its ability to collect an array of intelligence remotely – in broad terms, geospatial intelligence (imagery) and signals intelligence (communications of various types). This remote collection capability was especially important against the Soviet target, an inherently secretive state, with extensive internal security, and a large land mass often obscured by bad weather. A rough rule of thumb during the Cold War was that eighty percent of the needed intelligence was classified and twenty percent was open. These computer and collection technologies were essentially home grown within the intelligence community, built by trusted contractors, and vastly superior to anything that might exist in the non-classified world.

In 1943, Thomas Watson, the president of IBM, famously predicted, "I think there is a world market for maybe five computers." In 1977, Ken Olsen, the founder of Digital Equipment Corporation (DEC), said, "There is no reason anyone would want a computer in their home." Of course, neither man envisioned personal computers, which got smaller and more powerful over time, nor the Internet and Worldwide Web, which gave consumers, as opposed to computer hobbyists, a reason to purchase home computers. The intelligence community did not foresee these developments either. As computer technology evolved and a commercial consumer market emerged, the unilateral computer advantage enjoyed by intelligence agencies largely disappeared. Commercial information technology capabilities and offerings sometimes surpassed intelligence community capabilities. Indeed, the reversal was so severe that working-level US intelligence computer capabilities began to lag behind the commercial market by the mid-1990s, largely because of a time-consuming government acquisition process that made it difficult for intelligence agencies to buy the latest machines as well as the security requirements that had to be added to machines, costing further time and money and therefore limiting options due to a declining budget.

Similarly, intelligence imagery collection from space had been, initially, the duopoly of the United States and the Soviet Union. By the 1980s, other nations also had this capability, although with less frequent collection and with lesser resolution (image clarity). We now have the advent of a number of commercial capabilities not tied directly to any government programs as private-sector firms began offering space-based imagery. Once again, a significant intelligence technical advantage has been eroded not by ineptitude or sloth but by a series of commercial advances that were unforeseen.

This erosion of one-time unilateral technical advantages is one of the issues with which intelligence agencies must deal. This means that one of the unique points of entrée that intelligence once enjoyed no longer exists. Therefore, the ever elusive "value added" that intelligence officers seek to provide for policy makers must come from somewhere else, perhaps analysis. It also means that some of the basis for classification has also eroded, as more collection comes from commercial vice national systems.

Most writing about the various important technology trends gravitate to one of two poles: breathless hyperbole about all of the good things that will happen as this or that technology is adapted, or deep skepticism and perhaps unremitting gloom about the dangers inherent in each technology. Both are correct, of course. Again, much depends on how the technology is used and how it is regulated or controlled.

There are so many different technologies that are making rapid advances that offer both opportunities and challenges but much of the writing about this tends to focus on a smaller group, usually related to the explosion of data and efforts to deal with these data, which we will touch on here. It is also important to note that many of these developments are extremely inter-related and inter-dependent in terms of the promise or threat that they pose.

A good place to start is the annual DNI's Worldwide Threat Assessment. Early every year the DNI presents this global assessment in several public appearances before congressional committees. This assessment is the view of the most senior US intelligence official about the most pressing issues that he faces. (General James Clapper has characterized this annual presentation as "Doomint," meaning "doom intelligence," a litany of threats and warnings.) Although the preface to this assessment always notes that the issues are not presented in some sort of rank order, the position of issues in the assessment does change from year to year, suggesting at least an informal ranking. In 2016, as it had in several past years, cyber was the first issue. But in 2016 the issue was renamed "Cyber and Technology," a significant change.

DNI Clapper's lead paragraph noted that devices "designed and fielded with minimal security requirements and testing and an ever-increasing complexity of networks could lead to widespread vulnerabilities in civilian infrastructures and US Government systems. These developments will pose challenges to our cyber defenses and operational tradecraft but also create new opportunities for our own intelligence collectors." DNI Clapper's testimony goes on to cover most of the more prevalently discussed technologies.

The Internet of Things (IoT) refers to a convergence of wireless technology, very small electromechanical systems, and the Internet. In short, virtually any device can be constructed so that it connects to the Internet, providing information about its performance and allowing for both benign and hostile remote access and possibly control. Properly used, the internet of things is both benign and a convenience, such as the ability to monitor remotely the functioning of a cardiac pacemaker or for a vending machine to inform its supplier that it needs to be refilled. The internet of things also generates a great deal of data about the growing number of devices that are connected. (One estimate is that by 2020, fifty billion devices will be part of the internet of things.) However, the internet of things also creates vulnerability in that these devices can be attacked or potentially controlled remotely. For example, in 2013, former Vice President Dick Cheney said that his doctors had disabled the wireless capacity of his pacemaker so as to thwart the possibility of remote assassination. The October 2016 distributed denial of service (DDoS) attacks on Dyn, which disabled many popular websites, was accomplished by turning common devices connected to the Internet into thousands of robots that could unwittingly take part in the attack.

As more and more everyday devices become part of the internet of things, intelligence agencies will have to be careful about examining these devices before they are brought into secure sites. In 1999, NSA banned Furbies, small robotic toys with infrared ports; Furbies appeared to "learn" English over time as their programmed vocabulary went from "Furbish" to English. Undetected collectors or transmitters pose an obvious threat to any intelligence enterprise but it will likely not be practical to ban all such devices from being placed in intelligence agencies. There simply will be too many of them. At the same time, devices connected to the internet of things offer excellent opportunities to collect intelligence if a device that you control can be implanted. Data provided by these devices, if they can be accessed, could provide insights into energy usage; "patterns of life" (that is, understanding people's habits); overall economic vitality; or possibly how these societies are evolving and changing. There are search engines that can locate devices connected to the Internet either in bulk or by specific type.

The internet of things is but one source in an ever-increasing flow of data. Indeed, it is this vast amount of raw data produced across an Internet-connected world that drives many of the other potential technological vectors of change. But there is no simple starting point to describe these vectors because they are, as noted, highly inter-dependent.

If there is a starting point in this discussion of technological change then it is likely to be the data or, as they are usually called, "Big Data." DNI Clapper did not touch on big data in his threat assessment but it is an important area to consider. Few technological areas are more prone to the hyperbole noted above. The issue in dealing with big data goes beyond sheer size; there are also the issues of complexity, lack of structure, heterogeneity and the fact that the data stream never stops. Big data is typically defined as data that exhibits three main characteristics, the three Vs: volume, variety, and velocity. The data come in very large amounts and in a wide variety of types and forms and often lack any formal structure; and the data must be processed quickly, at least when being used for intelligence. These factors all militate against the use of traditional data bases. Indeed, we turn to the importance of artificial intelligence, algorithms, and machine learning.

A key question to ask is: data about what? Enthusiasts will answer: everything! Data comes from various types of communications, social media, the internet of things, and virtually any device connected to or record created on a system that is connected to the Internet or Worldwide Web. For example, there are ten billion cell phone calls and one hundred billion emails sent daily. So, the answer about the data – "everything" – is accurate but that is not comforting to many intelligence professionals. Several writers on intelligence, including myself, have noted that there is a very large and important difference between information and intelligence. Information is anything that can be known about anything. Intelligence focuses on the information that is of importance to policy makers – by definition a much smaller set. So, big data in and of itself is not likely to be interesting or important in terms of intelligence. One has to do something with it. Given the choice, most intelligence professionals would rather have more data than less but not necessarily if this means a veritable flood of data, much of which is not relevant or useful. Moreover, there may be types of data that may be kept from intelligence services for reasons of privacy, limitations in their charters, data that are considered proprietary, and so on. It is likely, therefore, that limits will be set on how much data is used by intelligence agencies based on its relevance or utility, or various legal limitations.

If we accept the "everything" starting point when thinking about big data and intelligence, then the first issue to consider is: Where are the data coming from? How will intelligence agencies get access to it? Very little attention appears to have been paid to this fundamental question, in part because of the underlying assumption that the owners of the data will be the people who are analyzing it. That may be true for financial institutions, social media outlets, utilities, and so on, but it will not be true for intelligence agencies. Someone controls or owns these data. There is an irony here for US intelligence, which has striven for years to get away from the concept of "data ownership" when referring to its own collected intelligence, which implies that the agency that collected the intelligence has the ultimate authority to decide how it will be used and by whom. This has been expressed by the word ORCON on a piece of intelligence, meaning "originator controlled," or to indicate that the agency first producing and disseminating the intelligence has continuing control over its further use. This ownership stance was an obvious obstacle to information sharing. Instead, the intelligence community moved by stages from data ownership to data stewardship and, finally, under DNI Mike McConnell, to "responsibility to provide," meaning that the agencies that collected the intelligence had and have a positive obligation to share it with those who need it. That said, the ORCON designation still survives.

But in the case of data or big data, ownership is an issue. Much of the data being discussed, such as the internet of things or public utility or financial or social media data will likely be proprietary. The data are not just sitting somewhere waiting to be analyzed by whoever wants access to them. For the entities who own the data these are both a valuable resource that will enable them to operate more efficiently and perhaps make money from the data and also something that they have a responsibility to safeguard. Will intelligence agencies access these data by a straightforward request, or by a court order, or surreptitiously – beg, borrow, or steal, if you will? If the data are owned by a US entity or contain information about US persons, then the rules for access are more stringent than if they were foreign data. Moreover, given the current disjuncture between the private sector and intelligence agencies as seen in the rift between Apple and the FBI in the aftermath of the San Bernardino shootings, a cooperative relationship and sharing seems unlikely. An alternative means would be to have intermediaries who are given some limited range of access and who analyze the data and then pass it to the intelligence agencies. But this assumes, again, that the data owners would be willing to do this and that the intelligence agencies would trust these intermediaries to do the data analysis.

Once we are past the not insignificant issue of access to the data, we need some methodology in order to filter it reliably, allowing data analysts and more traditional intelligence analysts to focus on the most promising data sets. Some big data advocates will take exception to this approach, arguing that we have, at the outset, denied ourselves the very promise of big data: the ability to discover hitherto unknown patterns or correlations. This may be true in the abstract but there is no capacity within intelligence to deal with "all" of the data. Some choices have to be made about which data to analyze now, which to analyze later if time allows, and which to set aside completely. Again, this admittedly runs counter to the approach preferred by big data advocates but it is the only practical way to proceed. Intelligence agencies have already been grappling with this issue but they are likely to arrive at answers that will be unsatisfactory to the data analytics "purists."

To some degree this filtering issue has been solved in terms of how devices connected to the Internet receive and sort incoming data. There is a series of protocols, a protocol stack, that breaks down, sorts, and distributes incoming data based on which data need to go where in the stack. There are either four or seven layers, depending on the model being used. However, this routing and transmission function may not be totally analogous to what may be needed for big data to be of ultimate use to intelligence analysts.

Setting aside the important issue of filtering the data, there are several other still nascent but developing tools and capabilities that become important. Again, it is difficult to discuss them one by one because they are highly inter-connected and interdependent.

A good beginning point is artificial intelligence (AI), a term coined by programmer John McCarthy in 1955. Artificial intelligence is traditionally defined as the ability of machines to execute tasks or solve problems as humans do. Artificial intelligence can mean speech recognition programs like iPhone's Siri or self-driving cars. Chroniclers of artificial intelligence note that there was a sixty year drought in AI developments. The recent renewed surge has been brought about by another convergence of disparate capabilities: cheap parallel computing, which allows the creation of neural networks that interact to make sense of received signals; more available data; and better algorithms, which allow the neural networks to "learn" faster as the data moves through them. This learning aspect is very important in artificial intelligence as one of the overall goals is for machines to continue to acquire these capabilities. Google's search engine or IBM's Watson program, which defeated two *Jeopardy!* quiz masters, are both examples of artificial intelligence overall and, especially, the ability to "learn" over time.

There are still limits to artificial intelligence. Machines can recognize specific objects, for example, but they cannot make intuitive associations about them. For example, in the 1980s, when I worked at the State Department's Bureau of Intelligence and Research, we were quite excited to discover baseball fields in Luanda, Angola, confirming the presence of Cuban troops. A machine can discover baseball fields from imagery; it can also list all of the countries that enjoy baseball (the United States, Canada, Mexico, Japan, and several in Latin America). But it cannot undertake the political analysis necessary to eliminate everyone but the Cubans as likely being present in Angola.

Artificial intelligence is actually a series of different goals – such as deduction, knowledge presentation, planning, and so on – pursued by many different tools. The promise of artificial intelligence is the ability to free humans from tasks that may seem mundane or that machines can do better. Watson, for example, is now used to assist in medical diagnoses. The most-oft cited threat in artificial intelligence is the revolt of the robots like the homicidal computer HAL in the movie *2001: A Space Odyssey* or the robots in the film version of Isaac Asimov's *I, Robot*. Although dramatic, these concerns are very far off. The more immediate concerns are false data or corrupt algorithms that can cause great damage. In his threat assessment, DNI Clapper cited the example of automatic stock trading programs, or the ability either to attack or to gain control of artificial intelligence systems via cyber space. Once again, this potential threat can also be an opportunity either to gain control of an adversary's artificial intelligence system or to feed it corrupt data. Every device connected to the Internet can be both an intruder and a target.

Let us posit that a nation is able to gain access to the missile command and control system of a potentially hostile state, at least to the point of raising questions about the reliability of that system. Would that be good or bad? It would depend on how the affected state reacted. The state might decide to stand down its systems to test them. It might embark on a new weapons acquisition program to overcome the problem. Or it might even decide to launch missiles, without concern as to their efficacy, in response to what it saw as a hostile act. Getting access is only part of the issue. Positing likely effects of that access will also matter, especially to policy makers.

Artificial intelligence is, in turn, dependent on advances in machine learning, essentially the ability of computers to learn without being specifically programmed. The learning involves the ability to deal with big data sets and derive previously unsuspected patterns and to do so with increasing capability over time. The 2015 victory of the AlphaGo computer program over professional Go player Lee Sedol is an example of a machine that was able to learn. The future of machine learning is, in turn, dependent on neural networks, combining multiple machines to assist in computation, akin to human neural networks.

Several issues arise concerning the relative promise of the data and the tools required to make sense of the data. The first one, noted above, is the question of what data we are working with and why. Big data advocates argue that one of the attractions of big data is the possibility of discovering hitherto unknown correlations and patterns within the data, hence the very need to analyze the data. Some will cite the counter-terrorist programs that seek to make connections between seemingly disparate and unconnected individuals. This is a valid example of how large data sets can be successfully queried but it remains narrow and highly focused, a far cry from the more random searches sometimes advocated. That said, machines do have an advantage in that they are less likely to use or reject data based on various cognitive biases – of which there are a great many and to which all analysts are subject from time to time.

This vagueness at the core of some big data arguments is problematic. Jennifer Dutcher, who works at Berkeley's School of Information's online masters in data science program, interviewed forty data analytics thought leaders. Among the more striking comments were that big data analytics was used when one did not know what questions to ask; that big data need to be transformed to be of value; and "collect now, sort later." These views run counter to how intelligence enterprises work. Although major intelligence agencies have long collected more intelligence than they ultimately process and exploit and pass along to analysts, they still focus their collection on the areas of greatest interest or concern. For example, Russia or Iran will always get much more collection than will Argentina. There appears to be a much more random aspect to the amassing of big data and a view that collecting ever more data is not only a benefit but is essential. Intelligence agencies would prefer to collect more than less if at all possible but even then it is not collection for the sake of collection. "Collect now and sort later" is also contrary to the necessary timelines against which intelligence operates. The "now" imperative is not only "collect" but also "analyze." There is a cumulative effect and benefit to collecting intelligence over time, which most intelligence agencies do, of aggregating the collected intelligence and looking back at as much of it as possible. But there is no allowed luxury of postponing analysis for some later date.

There is nothing new about intelligence agencies collecting and using data. Economic performance, weapons development, pandemics, and many other issues all depend on data. But this is a far cry from the transformative promises of big data evangelists. There is almost an *X-Files* sense to this random search: "The truth is out there." That may not be so. This vague and random search based on data may also prove difficult to justify on a large-scale basis for intelligence agencies whose budgets are constrained. They must focus on the issues of highest priority and concern. A better solution may be for intelligence agencies to keep in close contact with the private sector and then buy and adapt successful tools and techniques – assuming that the private sector will be amenable to such relationships. This has become an issue in recent years, as we will discuss in Chapter 4.

One of the central questions when dealing with any intelligence is its reliability. Is the human source truthful, a fabricator, or a double agent, sent to deceive? Has the collected image or signal been subject to deception of some sort? Big data would appear to raise these same questions, only in some larger regard. As noted, DNI Clapper raised the issue of data reliability. Given the vulnerability of most networks and the large amounts of data being collected from very varied sources, how can we ascertain its reliability? One senior intelligence official has suggested assigning confidence levels to data just as is done with human intelligence today ("a reliable source with access"; "an untested source with unknown access"; and so on). In human intelligence, these qualifiers are provided by reports officers who have working knowledge of the source. But when dealing with data the confidence issues become more complex and more difficult. Who will assign the confidence level: those dealing with the data or those analysts receiving it? They are likely to have very different assessments, just as analysts tend to have varying degrees of preference for this or that collection discipline based, in part, on their home agency. For example, when I worked at the State Department's Bureau of Intelligence and Research I noticed that CIA analysts tended to put greater reliance on human sources than we did, while we valued diplomatic reporting more than some CIA analysts. How you analyze depends, in part, on where you sit.

There is also the risk that erroneous data will get into a set or into the broader intelligence system and may not be discovered for some time, if at all. In computer science this is sometimes called the GIGO problem: garbage in, garbage out. But here is a real-world example of the problem from the run up to the second war with Iraq: Curveball. Curveball was the name given to an Iraqi who defected to Germany in 1999. He claimed to be a chemical engineer with knowledge of mobile biological weapons laboratories in Iraq. Curveball was under the control of German intelligence and the German service denied the request of the US Defense Intelligence Agency (DIA) to have Curveball take a very short polygraph to determine his reliability. German officials later claimed that they warned about their own concerns about Curveball's reliability. DIA did make use of the information provided by Curveball; DIA analysts then shared this intelligence with their colleagues in other agencies who were also working on the Iraq WMD issue – exactly as they had been trained to do.

When it was later determined that Curveball had been lying, Director of Central Intelligence George Tenet asked me to find out how we had gone astray on this source. The answer lay in the sharing of intelligence. Once inaccurate intelligence got into the system, or systems, it became difficult to track down everyone who had received it and might be working from it. When DIA realized that Curveball was not a reliable source, the agency put out a "burn notice," warning analysts not to use Curveball's information. However, not all analysts were aware of the burn notice, in part because the intelligence sharing system is at some levels informal and personal, as one would expect. During the stress of a very busy period – the obvious approach of war – some analysts did not relay the burn notice to colleagues with whom they had shared Curveball's reporting. Analysts are trained to share useful intelligence with other analysts, including colleagues in other agencies, who are working on the same issue. Indeed, the failure to share intelligence was one of the criticisms levelled against US intelligence in the so-called 9/11 Commission Report. But there is likely not going to be a central log of everyone who has received and is working on certain intelligence sources because the intelligence sharing system is at some level personal and informal. This is a strength in terms of overall intelligence analysis but not in terms of record keeping.

I reported back to Tenet that we had made some changes to improve the burn notice system but I also said, "At best, it will be about ninety-seven percent effective. The good news is that we shared intelligence; the bad news is that we shared bad intelligence."

Again, these same vulnerabilities of data may also translate into operational possibilities when dealing with the data sets and systems of hostile states, the ability to insert bad data into someone else's system. But here we need to be careful about which systems we corrupt. We have to be concerned about "blowback," that the corrupted data will travel back and infect our systems as well. There may be less danger of blowback if we corrupt a state's military command and control system (although there are other ramifications to worry about here) than if we corrupt the Iraqi banking system. To cite an actual example, in the period before the First Gulf War (1990–91), US policy makers considered attacking Iraq's banking system to prevent

Saddam Hussein from buying new weapons if the war was a prolonged one. But someone then asked: Are not the Iraqi banks connected to other Middle Eastern banks? And are not those banks connected to the global banking system? What might be the effects? Given these uncertainties, the Iraqi banks were not touched.

Another issue is the reliability of the correlations or patterns that are derived. As has been often pointed out, correlation is not causation. Ashleigh Brilliant, an author and cartoonist, may have put it best, "My sources are unreliable, but their information is fascinating." Again, there is likely to be a gap between data scientists and "old style" analysts (admittedly, a passing breed) when it comes to giving credence to derived correlations. But this issue will also extend to policy makers, as will be discussed in Chapter 3.

Finally, some of the intelligence issues most important to policy makers – and, therefore, to intelligence analysts – are unlikely to be useful fields for big data analytics. Leadership intentions is one of the most important and difficult issues sought by policy makers. Why is Vladimir Putin acting as he is? What are his near and long-term goals? Worse still, what about leaders whose very rationality appears to be questionable or at least extremely difficult to understand, such as Muammar el-Qaddafi or Kim Jong Un? Or, to take a much debated case, Saddam Hussein and weapons of mass destruction (WMD). Saddam told the truth in 2002, a rare enough event, when he said that Iraq did not have WMD. Why then did he not allow inspections to forestall a US-British attack? It would appear to be the most logical response since he had nothing to hide. But it is likely that both national pride and a fear of Iran led him to make a decision that assured he would face a losing war. No amount of data analytics could have squared the circle between Saddam's statements and his behavior and the resulting US–British decision to go to war.

Similarly, political surprise is a reality that most policy makers hope to avoid and look to their intelligence officers to minimize and to give sufficient warning. But the ratio of successful warning to major unexpected political surprise is probably not very good: Richard Nixon goes to China; Anwar Sadat goes to Israel; F. W. De Klerk decides to free Nelson Mandela and negotiate an end to apartheid. It would have been the very rare – and likely disbelieved analyst – who would have forecast any of these events in the years or even months prior to their occurring. For one thing, these decisions were made in secret and were largely the result of assessment and decisions made by a single individual, who would likely be unwilling to share his radical plans very widely lest they arouse determined opposition and leaks designed to kill the concept.

No amount of big data analytics would have forewarned about these events, either, unless one begins to believe in the fictional "psychohistory" posited by Isaac Asimov in his *Foundation* series. As Karl Spielmann, a former CIA senior analyst, points out ("I Got Algorithm: Can There Be a Nate Silver in Intelligence?", *International Journal of Intelligence and Counterintelligence*, 29, 525–44, 2016), there are no analytical models or data sets upon which such political analyses can be based.

Where does this leave us in terms of technology and the future of intelligence?

- We clearly live in a more inter-connected and data-driven world. Both of these factors will grow in intensity over time. There will be more machines and devices connected to the internet of things producing more data. But not all of these data will be of interest or use to intelligence analysts.
- The interconnectivity has created both vulnerabilities for society in general, such as potential attacks on infrastructure, and for intelligence specifically, in terms of the inherent vulnerabilities of systems connected in some way to the Worldwide Web, which become subject to intrusion, data manipulation or leaking.

- However, these vulnerabilities also become opportunities if they can be exploited in the intelligence systems of other states.
- There is a middle ground between the optimistic big data analytic advocates and the extreme skeptics. Interestingly, many senior intelligence officers interviewed for this book occupy this middle ground, recognizing the likely utility of some aspects of big data analytics but seeking various means – such as up-front filtering, confidence levels – to make the analyzed data actually useful. For intelligence, big data analytics and the underlying technologies – artificial intelligence, machine learning, and neural networks – remain very nascent works in progress. It may also be that, at least for intelligence analysis, big data will be like cold fusion in physics, something whose promise is always in the offing.

A final technological issue that must be addressed is the wider issue of cyber space itself. It has become almost banal to discuss the vulnerabilities inherent in cyber space for intelligence agencies or anyone else. (Cyber space is discussed more fully in Chapter 4.) But several points are worth noting:

- First, the information technology upon which we rely was not built to provide secure means of banking, commerce, or communications. So, at the core of the cyber-space issue we have a mismatch of means and ends, and no one seems willing to go back and create a new, more secure worldwide cyber environment. Too many government and private-sector enterprises have been unwilling to do the most basic things needed to secure sensitive data.
- Second, we have never before seen a technology capable of mass disruption, if not destruction, especially against infrastructure, that was so readily available to anyone. The barrier to entry is the

ability to buy a personal computer, sign on to an internet service provider, and know some rather basic computer skills.

A major issue for intelligence agencies, as DNI Clapper points out in his 2016 threat assessment, is the ability of hostile intelligence services to analyze bulk data to identify intelligence officers. This was the inherent issue in the Chinese intrusion into the files of the US Office of Personnel Management (OPM) in 2015. Hostile states can compare the OPM data with the data provided about individuals posted to their country. If these two sets of data do not match, it might help identify officers who are under cover. Interestingly, in public testimony about the OPM breach, DNI Clapper was far from alarmist: Data was "simply stolen. That's a passive intelligence collection activity – just as we do."

Beyond that are the issues of cyber-space threat, warning, and vulnerability, which will be discussed in Chapter 4.

DNI Clapper listed Russia and China as the main cyber threats, followed by Iran, North Korea, and several non-state actors. What is left unsaid, of course, is an assessment of US capabilities in cyber space, which most analysts believe to be superior to anyone else. So, again, the cyber-space issue cuts both ways, a threat and an opportunity.

The other aspect of intelligence where technological change matters a great deal is intelligence collection. The ability to collect intelligence that is not readily available and that cannot be obtained elsewhere has always been a core or bedrock activity and source of both power and entrée for intelligence agencies and officers. The phrase "knowledge is power" can be traced as far back at the sixth century CE in some Shi'a texts, although, as noted in Chapter 1, in an authoritarian state too much knowledge can also be extremely dangerous. But, as will be discussed in Chapter 3, intelligence managers aspire to be more than the keepers of the keys to crucial collection secrets.

There are five major types of intelligence collection, sometimes referred to as collection disciplines or INTs:

- HUMINT: human intelligence, meaning both espionage and openly collected intelligence from human sources.
- GEOINT: geospatial intelligence, a descendant of what had been called IMINT, or imagery, but that now embraces more than just photos.
- SIGINT: signals intelligence, meaning all sorts of communications, between people or between machines (such as radars and weapons tests).
- MASINT: measurement and signatures intelligence, meaning an array of physical phenomenon that can be collected and identified, such as seismic waves (earthquakes or nuclear tests), nuclear radiation and electrical emanations.
- OSINT: open-source intelligence, meaning any information that is neither classified nor proprietary.

Many who write about collection will refer to GEOINT, SIGINT, and MASINT as the technical intelligence collection types but in reality each of the five types of collection has an important technical component. And each of these collection disciplines faces technological challenges and opportunities.

Human intelligence can involve various technologies to support collection or to exfiltrate collected intelligence but the most important technological change for this branch of collection may be the increasing difficulty in establishing cover, the false identity used by human intelligence officers when they are working overseas. Again, these difficulties have come about because of changes in technology or social trends elsewhere; it is not a case of intelligence officers being unaware of or resistant to change. It is a case of technology creating new impediments and new opportunities.

Case officers have typically traveled under false passports, which are not that difficult to create, whether it is a passport from their nation or someone else's. The International Civil Aviation Organization (ICAO) began working on the issue of machine readable travel documents in the late 1960s. By 2001, a great deal had been accomplished but the terrorist attacks against the United States that year using commercial passenger airplanes gave new impetus to the concept. Most of the world's nations have now agreed to issue e-passports or biometric passports, which contain a microprocessor chip and some sort of biometric identifier (face, fingerprint or iris recognition). Critics of the program have cited numerous instances in which the security features of the new passports can be defeated; others have cited civil liberty concerns.

For intelligence agencies the question is more basic: how do you establish and maintain a false identity that is dependent on unique biometric data? As a means of identifying potential agents coming into one's country under a false identity the biometric passports are a plus. In terms of posting agents abroad, they are a significant problem.

The second problem affecting cover is the rise of social media, which is a very recent phenomenon. Facebook became open to anyone over the age of thirteen in 2006. Instagram was launched in 2010. As of the second quarter of 2016, Facebook had 1.71 billion active monthly users, or just under a quarter of the world's population. The odds are very good, therefore, that someone being recruited to join the Clandestine Service will have a Facebook page, and may have had one for as long as ten years. Therefore, these would-be recruits have an established public presence and profile going far beyond their immediate circle of family, friends, and colleagues. In order for this person to go under cover, this social media profile creates a problem. First, they cannot be using Facebook, at least in their true name, when they are sent out to their post. That person, the true name person, does not exist in that country. Second, it is probably best if they do not cease using Facebook entirely (sometimes referred to as "Facebook suicide") lest people with whom they are in contact wonder where they are or what has become of them. Third, should not their cover persona have a Facebook account? Will it seem strange or out of place if they do not? If they create a false name account, what about face recognition software that could cross-reference the two accounts? These issues are undoubtedly manageable but difficult, presenting a very different set of challenges for the practice of the "world's second oldest profession."

On the other hand, social media may prove to be a useful tool for some types of HUMINT recruitment. The Islamic State has had some success recruiting volunteers over social media. There will be concerns about the reliability of individuals recruited in this manner, operational security, and the issue of possible deception but there may be some HUMINT opportunities as well. Social media can also provide information about individuals that once required direct contact, as long as we are alert to the possibility of deception. Some years ago the *New Yorker* magazine ran a cartoon showing two dogs sitting at a computer. One dog says to the other, "On the Internet, no one knows you're a dog."

A countervailing technology may be found for human intelligence operators in virtual reality. Virtual reality allows the creation of a real or imaginary setting with which an individual can interact. Assuming the data are available, spaces in which human intelligence operators will be working can be created, allowing the agent to familiarize himself or herself with the setting, entry and exit points, and so on. This has obvious operational benefits and may provide another venue for human recruiting by enticing potential sources into an attractive shared virtual reality.

Geospatial intelligence used to be called imagery, or even photographic intelligence. But there is a significant difference. Briefly, geospatial intelligence means not just the image and what we see in it but also physical activities, human geography, and a host of other data that may be associated with the image. The geography application on most mobile phones offers many of these features. You can get a map of where you are or an image, traffic conditions, transit lines, and so on. All of these are part of geospatial intelligence.

As noted, there was a time when geospatial intelligence, initially the ability to take pictures of the Earth via orbiting satellites, was a duopoly. Only the United States and the Soviet Union could do this. But there has been a fairly widespread democratization of this intelligence capability, not only among nation states but in the commercial sector, some of whose satellites offer rather detailed imagery. For example, DigitalGlobe's WorldView-4 satellites offer panchromatic (black and white imagery) with a resolution of 0.31 meters (just over 12 inches), meaning objects of that size or larger can be identified in an image, and 1.24 meters (almost 5 feet) resolution in multispectral imagery.

This loss of exclusivity is only one of the change vectors. Another is in the nature of issues that face policy makers and thus their intelligence agencies. Not all issues involve military forces or even nation-based activities. Transnational issues like pandemics or refugee flows are now more prominent parts of the policy and intelligence portfolios and therefore become intelligence requirements, albeit very different from the classic national security issues and much less reliant upon classified – as opposed to open – intelligence.

This creates a severe challenge for intelligence agencies. Exquisite or compelling imagery has always been one of the easiest means of gaining entrée to a policy maker. Moreover, imagery has always had an advantage in that it does not need to be explained in terms of how it was obtained. It is just a camera of sorts, after all. (This does not obviate the requirement for photo interpreters, who are often needed to explain what is being seen in the image that may be obscure or difficult to identify to the untrained eye.) No longer being the exclusive provider of geospatial intelligence entails a loss. But it also suggests a gain. Not all geospatial intelligence demands require the most exquisite image or most capable satellite, especially some of the transnational issues noted above. For example, at the outset of the US campaign in Afghanistan in 2001, then-NGA Director James Clapper bought all rights in perpetuity for imagery of Afghanistan taken by the Ikonos satellite, then operated by Space Imaging, and now part of DigitalGlobe. This gave NGA access to one-meter (just over three feet) and four-meter (13 feet) resolution, which would be sufficient for certain requirements, thus supplementing NGA's overall collection capability. It also kept this stream of commercial imagery out of the hands of anyone trying to track US and then coalition forces via this imagery. During the ebola outbreak in West Africa, the National Geospatial-Intelligence Agency released "geospatial layers" about cultural places and structures, and a range of infrastructure data that would be important in supporting the medical efforts to combat the disease. These data were posted on websites and updated regularly so relief workers could keep current.

This brings us to a point where we have to reconsider what is meant by geospatial intelligence. It may not be an image at all but a collection of data that has a geographic nexus and can be represented in some visual form. Technology that tracks social media posts, for example, can display expressed opinions by location and frequency. This has a geospatial aspect but it is not imagery per se.

There are two trends occurring here. First, the geospatial mission is expanding in terms of how it collects and how it uses its intelligence. Second, it also means that at least part of the geospatial intelligence mission is not based on classified sources. The National Geospatial-Intelligence Agency has actually embraced this change, creating a project called Pathfinder that relies exclusively on a range of unclassified sources. These are important developments and indicate why the definition of geospatial intelligence is more than just imagery.

If the geospatial intelligence collectors no longer have a unilateral capability they must seek other ways to remain a viable part of intelligence. That is part of the drive in expanding the geospatial intelligence mission. But it also suggests that the often elusive "value add" that intelligence officers seek to provide to policy makers may have to shift "downstream" from the actual collected image to better and more meaningful analysis, which will be discussed more fully in Chapter 3.

A final shift to be discussed in geospatial intelligence stems from the broader definition of this intelligence versus its imagery forebears. Geospatial analysts use some types of imagery, such as video feeds from drones to establish what they call "patterns of life" or "activity-based intelligence (ABI)." These are both what intelligence analysts call indicators that serve to alert analysts either to activities that seem out of the norm for that location or that are generally known to indicate certain activities, such as the placement improvised explosive devices (IEDs). Obviously, such intelligence requires the compilation of data against which to make these analytic judgments and, of course, there will always be some room for doubt and for error. But pattern of life or activity-based intelligence are important indicators of the way in which geospatial intelligence is broadening its scope and relying on new analytic techniques.

One of the main issues facing signals intelligence, at least when discussing human communications, is similar, if not identical, to the data issues noted above: volume, variety, and velocity. Cryptography, broadly defined as the making and breaking of codes, dates to ancient history. Modern cryptography is often dated to World War I and the interception of international cable traffic, most notably in Britain's interception and coy disclosure to the United States of Germany's January 1917 offer to Mexico of a wartime alliance against the US, the Zimmermann Telegram. The practice actually began much earlier. Union and Confederate forces intercepted one another's telegram traffic during the American Civil War in the 1860s by tapping into telegraph wires. Telephone wiretapping dates back to at least the

1890s. Today, the available means of communicating have exploded: landline phones and mobile phones, emails, text messages, multiple social media platforms. Added to this is the widespread ability to encrypt communications, which may involve no more than buying a commercially available mobile phone that comes with enhanced encryption, or to hide one message in another (steganography). For signals intelligence, this "target rich" environment obviously cuts two ways: many places to look for communications and many places in which to hide them.

Not surprisingly, many of the technologies discussed earlier in this chapter related to data and its use are highly relevant to the future of signals intelligence. Just as with data, a key issue in signals intelligence has been filtering: identifying which signals sources are most important or most valuable; winnowing down the vast number of signals to those that are most likely to have the intelligence that is being sought; and then working through those signals (decrypting where necessary; translating from foreign languages) to produce initial intelligence. Word search programs can abet this effort. This was also the essence leaked by Edward Snowden. This program created a secure repository of telephone metadata (the fact of communications: which telephones were in contact, when) but not the actual contents of the communications. If a telephone number was subsequently determined, based on reasonable suspicion, to be associated with foreign terrorist activity, then the repository could be queried. Robert Litt, the general counsel for the DNI, aptly said, "If you want to look for a needle in a haystack, you have to start with a haystack." (There is the related issue of the declining willingness of commercial providers to cooperate with intelligence agencies, which will be discussed in Chapter 4.)

In January 2014, as part of his response to the Snowden leaks, President Obama signed Presidential Policy Directive 28: *Signals Intelligence Activities*, setting forth US policy in this area. The PPD also called for a series of reports on the governance of signals intelligence, including whether software could substitute for bulk collection. A study was conducted by the National Research Council, which is part of the National Academy of Sciences. This report, *Bulk Collection of Signals Intelligence: Technical Options*, concluded that no software technique would be a full alternative to for bulk collection when it is used to query records after the targets become known as there would be no historical repository. The report said that software might provide a more limited substitute in some other circumstances.

Machine translation, the ability of a machine to hear or read a language and translate those words into an understandable phrase or sentence in another language, is of obvious benefit to communications intelligence analysts. There are actually multiple ways to approach the problem of machine translation (including dictionary based, statistical, example based, rule based, and several others), and the field has made advances in recent years, although not to the point where any system is entirely reliable.

The competing vectors in communications intelligence are rather clear: many means of communications resulting in many ways to attempt to avoid interception or unwanted access. Signals intelligence is, to some degree, a constant dynamic of hiding versus seeking.

Measurement and signatures intelligence, MASINT, has been one of the least understood of the intelligence disciplines for several reasons. First, much of what happens to derive MASINT from its sources – the processing and exploitation – is rather arcane, especially when compared to any of the other INTs. Second, the technology from which MASINT is derived is not unique to it as are geospatial and signals. Indeed, much of MASINT is derived from these other two disciplines, and some have suggested that MASINT is not a separate INT at all but rather a by-product. The view here is that, the sources notwithstanding, MASINT presents unique intelligence with unique requirements and uses.

The major challenge facing MASINT brings us back to data, once again. MASINT collection is based on large amounts of data to allow the identification and exploitation of physical phenomena. The libraries of MASINT data are already large, and are growing in size. As MASINT exploitation of these data becomes increasingly detailed the data libraries become less wieldy unless the data are properly tagged before being put in the libraries. This turns, again, on the issue of the original size of the data set collected. Second, MASINT depends on many different types of data – electro-optical, geophysical, materials, nuclear, radar, radio frequency – that often have to be correlated with one another as part of the overall processing to create a composite signature. Correlating signatures across these vast libraries can be daunting. Finally, even within different parts of the MASINT community there may be variances as to how to measure collected data, making its shared utility more problematic.

On the positive side, the internet of things will provide a great deal of data that are of use to MASINT analysts. For example, as more people carry devices with unique radio frequency signatures, they become easier to identify and to track – although this again becomes a problem in human intelligence as we do not want our clandestine officers to be easily tracked. Advances in biometrics also offer additional signatures that will again cut both ways. Improvements in MASINT sensors allow greater discrimination between types of emanations at greater distances; the cost of sensors is also decreasing allowing occasional saturation approaches to MASINT targets. So, once again, we face the issue of data access.

There has been an explosion in the number and availability of open sources. There are several contributing factors:

- The end of the Cold War, which shifted several countries from closed societies to open ones.

- The growth of twenty-four news services and the ability of news providers (hard copy and broadcast) to make their content available on the Internet with near-continuous updates.
- The growth of social media.

That said, open source remains something of the "redheaded step child" of intelligence collection. Open source tends to receive more lip service than outright support or recognition among intelligence agencies and officers, who tend to show a preference for classified sources. Technology to "crawl" through multiple news sites is not that difficult; changing attitudes about open source is.

Keeping abreast of all of the news sources noted above can be daunting but is not technologically impossible. Social media is arguably the greatest challenge for open-source intelligence collection. The ubiquity of social media makes it an important intelligence source. But sheer volume can also be a problem, as noted with other collection disciplines. As with signals intelligence, there are both useful externals (the "fact of" social media being used, how many postings, and so on) and internals (what is being said by whom). In some respects, the internals may be more important, as they give the content and insights into what is prompting the use of social media. The internals can also help identify who, among the thousands of users, are the thought leaders. But one also has to be alert to the possibility that people will misrepresent who they are, may be *agents provocateurs*, or may have purchased phantom followers to boost their assumed importance. As noted, social media also has a geospatial intelligence function, in that social media posts can be analyzed in terms of location, giving some sense of local sentiments and areas of activism. There are several commercial providers who can geolocate and translate social media posts in near-real time. Finally, when collecting against social media sources some sort of cover will likely be necessary rather than reveal a connection with an intelligence agency. This, in turn, raises the issue of possibly collecting against US persons or perhaps even people in allied nations.

Anyone who understands open source will understand both the appeal and potential utility of social media. But, at the same time, this is a relatively new source that is not entirely understood in terms of its reliability and how to meld social media intelligence into broader intelligence analyses.

Even "fake news" – a new and somewhat oxymoronic phrase – has some analytic value. "Fake news" is really no different from the propaganda put out by authoritarian states. This tells you what the source wants you to believe even if the "news" is known to be fake, giving insight into their goals.

Open source, like any other intelligence source, must be processed and exploited. But in the case of open source it is not a technical activity to transform 0s and 1s into pixels or words but rather an understanding of the nature of the source and its inherent biases and agendas. For example, in the United States, MSNBC and *Fox News* rarely report the same news in the same manner; the same could be said for the *Guardian* and *The Daily Telegraph* in Britain. Bias does not automatically mean that a source has no value. Rather, if one understands the bias an analyst can then use that source to reflect one body of opinion. But the evaluation as to viewpoint, strength, and credibility still has to be made. As the world of open source continues to grow, this means that more time has to be spent benchmarking the sources before they can be used confidently.

This brief discussion of some of the intelligence collection disciplines suggests a number of potential change vectors.

- Secrecy. Collection capabilities have always been one of the main drivers of security classification. The need for secrecy as it relates to intelligence collection may diminish as more unclassified sources that are deemed reliable become available. This is certainly true for many aspects of geospatial and measurement and signatures intelligence, and should be true more generally if open source is accepted more warmly than it has been in the past. In the case of the internet of things, the fact of the search may remain classified but the techniques themselves are already unclassified and readily available.

Again, secrecy has lent a certain cachet to intelligence. Losing that cachet may not be entirely bad if intelligence agencies can find additional means of being useful to policy makers, especially in the analysis of the collected intelligence regardless of the source.

A decreased reliance on or need for secrecy will be a profound cultural change for intelligence agencies. On the other hand, if this perceived vector is correct it should also facilitate the greater use of intelligence between practitioners, as well as with policy makers, and perhaps with the public. This would also respond to calls for increased transparency on the part of intelligence agencies. More useful intelligence should be more attractive than highly classified intelligence. Indeed, if various prognostications about an ever more open world are correct, then the intelligence agencies that more quickly adjust to this change may have an advantage. This type of adjustment is also likely to be easier for intelligence agencies in democracies than in autocratic states, which inherently seek to place controls on all sorts of information.

- Competition. Intelligence collection agencies also have to deal with the fact that in many instances they have increasingly capable commercial or non-state actor competitors. Competition can be positive if it forces one to improve one's own efforts. But in the case of intelligence collection, especially in instances where the collection may be ambiguous or where collectors are still constrained by classification, there will now be alternative sources of information that can influence debates and policy deliberations, for either benign or malign reasons. Much will depend on who the competitive sources are, their reliability over time, and whether or not they have agendas of their own.

Disagreements between intelligence sources is nothing new; it is an inherent part of the business. Some of this may be resolved by trust in ongoing relationships between policy makers and their intelligence officers. But it is important to understand that, in democracies at least, there are likely to be many audiences beyond the policy makers: legislatures, media, the public. These alternative sources of intelligence may seek to influence these other audiences as a means of influencing policy.

- Denial and deception. The problems raised by competitive intelligence sources quickly lead into increased concerns about denial and deception, often referred to as D&D. Denial refers to hiding activities or objects from collection, such as building underground facilities, or timing them so as to avoid collection. Deception refers to misleading collection either by hiding or by displaying something that is actually false, such as the Allied deception operation prior to D-Day, called Operation Fortitude, which diverted German attention from the planned beachheads.

All intelligence collection is subject to doubt and to concerns about D&D. But these concerns are likely to increase as competitive sources of intelligence become more prevalent. There is an old CIA saying about newspapers: "Only the sports scores and weather are printed for information. Everything else is printed for effect." We can expand this somewhat cynical view to embrace any intelligence source but especially those not controlled by the intelligence agencies themselves.

For example, in the case of the increased use of open sources, such as NGOs for many transnational issues – such as pandemics, climate change, refugee flows – one has to understand that the NGOs are not neutral observers and reporters. They have agendas and preferred outcomes. Even if their goals are largely altruistic in nature, these may be at variance with policy makers' preferences or capabilities. They are likely going to present those facts or data that are most supportive of the outcome they prefer. The deception may not even be conscious; it may simply reflect the way in which they see and interpret a situation. But, again, this must be taken into account when using these sources.

- Data reliability. In a world driven by and dependent upon data, the reliability of that data becomes increasingly important. As we have noted, the various technologies that are part of the big data issue offer significant opportunities for intrusion and for data manipulation. How small or large does manipulated data have to be to corrupt a larger data set? Are the data sets so large that it will not matter or are they so sensitive that even small amounts of corrupt data will be a danger? There are several techniques and methodologies in existence to affirm data reliability. The question is their overall sensitivity and especially their ability to perform reliability testing quickly, which is always a major concern in intelligence.

- Redefining all source intelligence? There are different levels of intelligence: single source, multi-intelligence (usually referring to geospatial and signals being used together) and all source, meaning as many of the collection disciplines as are pertinent or available for a given issue. All source is the preferred goal when possible, because it is thought that by having multiple sources we are more likely to have a more accurate sense of what is happening. As noted, there are five acknowledged collection disciplines, some of which have sub-disciplines. Does the growing use of or reliance on data change that model?

One can argue that it does not. All collection is data of some sort and we are simply adding more data. However, the nature of these data, of big data, is in some respects different from the other INTs. Some experts argue that the data are a form of signals because they are largely derived from Internet traffic of various sorts, so are a result of communications, even if that communications is passive. One could also argue that the data are a form of MASINT because at least some of them, such as that derived from the internet of things, are incidental emanations of a sort. (Similar arguments have been made about cyber intelligence, which is currently treated as a form of signals.)

There are several reasons why this matters. The main reason has to do with the relationship of the analysts to collection overall and to the data specifically. There are aspects of the data that are extremely inferential, certainly when compared to other types of collection. The randomness of data collection, as noted above, and the acknowledged weaknesses of some correlations are important factors for analysts to consider when using these data. These very distinguishing aspects can be lost or subsumed when the data are seen as sub-sets of collection with which the analyst is familiar, even though the data have significant differences. As will be discussed in the next chapter, there may be differences between "traditional" analysts and data analysts when dealing with the data. It is best that these be examined, discussed, and debated, which is more likely to happen if the data are treated as a separate intelligence stream rather than as part of an already large collection, such as signals.

Finally, to be a bit bureaucratic, big data exists in a competitive budget environment. Each type of collection has its advocates; each type seeks more funding. Big data should be allowed to and required to make a case separate from the other disciplines if it is to be given an honest evaluation.

3

Analysis Vectors

Despite the popular images of satellites, spies, and covert operations, analysis is the main means by which intelligence interacts with policy makers. It may be impersonal, in the form of a written report, or it may be very personal, in the form of a briefing. But analysis – providing assessed intelligence to policy makers so they can reduce their uncertainty and perhaps achieve decision advantage, as noted in Chapter 1 – is the true mainstay of the intelligence–policy maker relationship. If there is a single point prediction in this volume it is this: that analysis will continue to be this central element in the policy–intelligence relationship. But how the analysis is achieved, about which topics, and by whom are all likely to be under some stress, in large measure as a result of the vectors already described.

The "holy grail" of intelligence analysis is not the correct forecast or prediction of what will happen next in any single event but the more nebulous concept of "value added." In intelligence this is an intellectual term, not an economic term. The intelligence analyst seeks to add value to the collected intelligence he or she receives, to explain context, significance, importance, and likely implications or results, which is then passed on to the policy maker. The original intelligence that prompted this analysis may or may not be passed along in the form in which it was collected, processed, and sent to the analyst. In some cases it may be appended to the analysis; in others it will simply be summarized and used as the starting point for the analysis that follows. But the emphasis here is on what the analyst adds to the collected intelligence.

Where does this value-added come from? In simplest terms it comes from the analyst's accumulation of knowledge and expertise and, presumably, his or her knowledge of the policy maker's interests, which are then turned into analytical insights. There are at least two key aspects to this value-added intelligence: meaning – what is this intelligence telling us, or not telling us; and likely outcomes – plural. It is very important to understand that this second aspect, likely outcomes, is not written in some dogmatic fashion of "given this intelligence, *this* is what will happen." That is not knowable and is likely a short course to disaster for the intelligence officer and the policy maker. There are usually multiple projected outcomes and these are written with more nuance and more uncertainty: "We see outcome A as most likely, and outcome B as less likely, and outcome C as least likely but still possible." To the layman or to the uninitiated policy maker this may seem like a rather pusillanimous approach. But the analyst is not hedging his or her bets to cover all possible outcomes. After all, the analyst cannot know with certainty which outcome will ensue. The key to this approach is the hierarchy of likelihood, giving the policy maker a sense of what to expect most or least so they can take whatever steps they deem appropriate on any or all of them.

This type of value-added intelligence need not come in response to an event or to newly collected intelligence. An important function for analysts is to provide analysis in anticipation of events or simply because there is either a perception or an understanding that this unrequested analysis may be of use to the policy makers.

In other words, the analyst seeks to be more – perhaps much more – than his or her collected intelligence. I referred to the intelligence value-add as a holy grail for several reasons. First, not all incoming intelligence lends itself to this. Some intelligence may be self-evident as to its implications or relatively unimportant and not worthy of the added effort, especially in a system where analysts are rarely available in abundance. Second, not all of the value-added aspects may be clear or clearly understood. The rationale for someone's actions or their implications may be difficult to discern or may be rejected out of hand as implausible even if they later turn out to be true. For example, the early US intelligence analysis of Nikita Khrushchev's policy towards Cuba in 1962 was that he would never be so reckless as to place missiles there. Such a step was certainly possible but it was not seen as being likely or plausible because Khrushchev had to know how the United States would react. But Khrushchev did not know or, rather, came away from his June 1961 meeting with John Kennedy convinced that he could overawe the President. So, in this case it took some time and more collected intelligence to convince analysts that Khrushchev had chosen what they saw as the riskiest policy, which they had seen as unlikely. Third, intelligence analysis is a risky business and not all analysts are willing to put themselves out on the high wire of analysis when it comes to value-added. Fourth, and perhaps most important, it is difficult to do and certainly difficult to do on a consistent basis. So, the holy grail of value-added does not happen all the time but it remains there, fixed in the minds of good intelligence analysts that this is their ultimate goal.

The fourth point above, the difficulty of consistent value-added, is important. During my tenure as the Assistant Director for Analysis at CIA, I read a copy of the President's Daily Brief (PDB) each day. There were days when the PDB seemed to be extremely well done, telling the President the types of intelligence that one would expect, major issues with trenchant analysis. On other days the

PDB seemed to be acceptable but not stellar. There were no days when it seemed to me to be below par. Each morning I would compare my reactions to the PDB with the senior intelligence officer responsible for overseeing it. I would say we agreed on which type of PDB it was – stellar or acceptable – at least ninety-five percent of the time. But the CIA officer said to me one day as we compared notes that at 4 am, when he was "putting the PDB to bed," he could not tell which one of the two types that morning's edition would be because he was so deeply involved in managing the process. He needed some distance to judge the PDB accurately. Another colleague of mine, who was a presidential briefer, put it this way, "I thought I had a really good morning in the Oval Office if I told the President something that he needed to know that he did not know before." But this may not happen every day. Indeed, this often becomes more difficult the longer the policy maker is in office, as he or she gains greater working familiarity with the issues and perhaps superior personal contacts with some of the foreign statesmen the intelligence officers are assessing.

Value-added intelligence is also dependent on the perception of the policy maker. Do they see the analysis as adding value for them? This depends on the knowledge of the policy maker – and especially if they know what they do not know, on their personality, and on their relationship with their intelligence officers. They may not see value-added in the same way. For example, analysis suggesting that a policy initiative is not working as planned, or that an adversary remains intractable, or that there is little that can be done to influence events in a given situation may be seen by the analyst as adding value but may be seen by the policy maker as unwarranted pessimism. In cases where different parts of the bureaucracy have staked out different positions on an issue, some policy makers may even accuse analysts of taking sides. So, value-added is in the eye of both the intelligence and the policy beholder, and their views may be quite different.

For intelligence to have value to policy makers it should be read, or briefed, with some regularity. There is no requirement in the US constitution for the President to have a daily intelligence briefing. Indeed, intelligence is not mentioned in the Constitution. But for policy makers to gain a certain facility and ease in dealing with issues they need regular exposure. This is why Donald Trump's statements prior to his inauguration that there was no need for him to be briefed every day because there was little new in each brief, and that he could get up to speed when necessary, were problematic. There is a cumulative effect in regular exposure to intelligence. It need not be every day (other Presidents also skipped some daily briefs) but many issues cannot be mastered and dealt with deftly on very short notice.

With these cautions noted, let us proceed on the basis that analysts wish to add value to intelligence as a means of assisting policy makers, and that policy makers will, at least some of the time, appreciate the effort if not the actual analysis itself.

Although adding value was and is difficult, it was less daunting when the majority of collected intelligence was secret, even if the goal of value-added analysis is to get beyond what has been collected. But, as noted in Chapter 2, today and in the future more collected intelligence is or will be unclassified, and there will be sources beyond the intelligence community offering information and assessments. Some of the basis for analysis may not be collected intelligence at all, either classified or unclassified, at least in the sense that these now exist. For example, this could be true of analyzed data, although the issue of how it is collected remains unresolved.

Even though analysts have always tried to be more than their intelligence sources, the transition to using more unclassified intelligence will also increase the burden in terms of bringing added value. Even though intelligence analysts are not in competition with the twenty-four news services, some policy makers may find it difficult to perceive a difference when intelligence has more open and less classified sourcing. For example, a President several administrations ago reportedly said to some intelligence officers who had just brought him some intelligence, "I just saw this on CNN. What do I need you for?" Therefore, the presumption is that in a world of less classified and more unclassified intelligence, the need to show value-added analysis will increase but may become more difficult.

One of the ways in which intelligence analysts could use open source intelligence to their advantage is to find and use new open sources about which the policy maker may be unaware. It is likely that intelligence analysts and certainly open source intelligence collectors will have much more time than will senior or even mid-level policy makers to identify new and useful open sources amidst the ongoing flood of information. The intelligence analysts may have to worry about the "I saw it on CNN" reaction or questions about future budgets but if they are being professionally honest there is something to be gained from bringing new and useful open sources to the attention of policy makers. However, as was noted in Chapter 2, open sources must be treated like all other intelligence sources, being vetted, exploited, processed, and assessed as to their validity, bias, and point of view. Even controlled open sources have some utility. For example, the Russian press under Putin parrots the official line but it is useful to know what that line is.

Another of the trends discussed previously, the increase in private firms providing intelligence, may also contribute to this value-added vector. For example, private imagery firms seek to sell more than the image. They also offer analytical services of various types. There are also numerous firms who either compete directly with intelligence services by marketing intelligence analysis on a broad range of international issues or risk-assessment firms producing mainly political or economic analysis for countries or regions. If we take a broad-minded and, I believe, correct view of these developments this competition should be seen as a benefit to future analytic efforts. Some of these firms may have strengths and expertise in areas that intelligence agencies do not, offering greater breadth of coverage.

But taking advantage of these providers may not come easy for intelligence agencies. Although they have had some contact and some professional relationships with some of these providers over time, there are several cultural inhibitions to doing so more often or on a broader basis. I suggested a similar broad outreach some years ago and was told by some colleagues that if we did this, then people who were not cleared would know what we were working on. I argued that if they were experts in their region or topic, they probably knew already and that they did not have to be cleared. After all, we were not telling them anything; they were telling us. Similarly, in 1996, when serving as staff director of the House Intelligence Committee, I wrote a provision that became part of the intelligence authorization act that year, giving the intelligence community authority to create a reserve from outside experts and to ask retiring officers if they would be willing to come back and serve for short periods if their expertise was needed. Although this became law, I was told by colleagues at CIA that it was not something they needed, and they would not use it. Interestingly, in the immediate aftermath of the 2001 attacks, President George W. Bush changed the retirement compensation rules to allow retirees who wanted to come back into service to do so without having their salary offset by deductions from their pensions. Bush said that he did not see why patriotic retirees should be penalized financially. So, there is likely an opportunity here but how it plays out depends on some cultural change.

There are also issues where secrecy simply is not an issue. Climate change is an excellent example. During his tenure as chairman of the House Intelligence Committee (2007–11), Representative Silvestre Reyes (D-NM), told DNI Mike McConnell that he wanted a national intelligence estimate written on climate change. McConnell argued, correctly, that this was not an issue that required classified intelligence sources and could be done outside of the intelligence community, but Reyes insisted. On September 21, 2016, President Barack Obama sent a memorandum to most of the Cabinet, the DNI, and several other agencies to "ensure that climate-change-related impacts are fully considered in the development of national security doctrine, policies, and plans." Most – but not all – people would recognize the critical nature of the issue but it is not one where classified intelligence is required. Indeed, the most knowledgeable experts on climate change are most likely to be found outside of the intelligence community. A similar observation could be made about infectious disease and pandemics. Demographics, which is a less dramatic issue but which is likely to have major effects in China, Russia, Japan, and some key countries in Europe, Africa, and the Middle East also relies largely on unclassified data. Interestingly, the Soviet Union began to misrepresent some of its demographic and health data during its later years to obscure overall declines in the quality of life and economics.

Outside sources and outside expertise becomes an opportunity, not a threat, allowing the intelligence agencies to have greater breadth and depth at no cost to other ongoing assignments. Analysts, aware of policy makers' concerns and of ongoing intelligence analysis, should have a better sense of which open source information will round out or add value to their analysis.

The likelihood that more intelligence analysis will be based on unclassified sources also raises the issue of whether these analyses should be more openly available. We would have to assume, for the time being, that we are discussing only those analyses that are entirely unclassified or those that have been declassified.

It should be noted that US intelligence agencies have been making more of their current intelligence papers available in recent years. The work that the National Geospatial-Intelligence Agency did regarding the ebola epidemic has been noted above. In addition, the National Intelligence Council (NIC) has been publishing its *Global Trends* papers, which look at macro trends that may shape the future some eight to fifteen years out, along with other analyses and reports from unclassified conferences that the NIC sponsors.

There are benefits to making intelligence analysis more "transparent," to use the popular parlance. (The larger issue of transparency will be discussed in Chapter 4.) First, these types of papers can be shared more easily with foreign governments. Second, the publication of analyses can serve to give legislative overseers, the media, and the public a better idea of what intelligence does and how it is written. There is a downside as well. Will those reading these analyses understand how to read them? Will they understand that these are not point predictions but a range of estimative forecasts? Reactions to the Intelligence Community Assessment (ICA) released in January 2017 concerning alleged Russian interference in the 2016 US election underscored each of these problematic responses. Some called for more specificity regarding sources; others had trouble understanding nuanced estimative language.

Finally, what will be the effect and potential cost when some of these analyses are inevitably shown to be wrong, as will occasionally be the case?

This problem of understanding what can often be highly nuanced language became apparent again in the aftermath of the 2002 national intelligence estimate on Iraqi weapons of mass destruction. Beyond the flaws in the analysis itself, I recognized that some of the people for whom we wrote did not understand our use of language. I asked Robert Walpole, one of the main drafters of the estimate, if we had ever written a glossary of estimative terms for policy makers to use. Walpole said that we had tried three times and no attempt had worked. I decided that we would try a fourth time. The ensuing paper, "What We Mean When We Say: An Explanation of Estimative Probability," now appears in every estimate and can be found online. Walpole's one-page paper takes the reader through a range of estimative probability and also confidence levels in judgments. Given that this paper is now an integral part of every estimate, and also appears in the January ICA on Russian election interference, I would judge it to be a success as an attempt to close this gap in understanding; but a lingering question remains: do policy makers ever read this page when looking at an estimate? There is no way of knowing.

One also has to consider the fact that all intelligence analysis is produced within a political system. During the latter part of the George W. Bush administration (2001–9), after the invasion of Iraq and the civil strife that ensued, there was considerable pressure exerted by Democrats in Congress for the publication of the key judgments of a succession of national intelligence estimates on the future of the conflict in Iraq. Key judgments are a summary of the major findings of the estimate and serve to give the busy reader a good sense of what the estimate says, minus much of the background analysis and supporting collection. As could be expected, those opposed to the President's policies would "cherry pick" the key judgments to find those statements that supported their views or their preferred policies.

Mike McConnell, the Director of National Intelligence at the time, reportedly told the President that he did not want to publish any more key judgments as they politicized the estimative process, were being misused, and that this was beginning to have a constraining effect on the analysts. President Bush agreed but the next national intelligence estimate to be completed was the November 2007 estimate, "Iran Nuclear Intentions and Capabilities." Despite his previous agreement, Bush ordered the key judgments of this estimate published, saying that they would eventually leak and likely be distorted, and therefore it was better to release an unclassified version that was authoritative. The key judgments of three more national intelligence estimates were released, after which the practice ended.

Thus, an increase in unclassified intelligence does increase the possibility of releasing more intelligence analysis but there are many other factors to be considered when doing so. One must always be mindful of the fact that intelligence analysis exists in a political arena and not in some abstract intellectual salon. Intelligence analysts strive and usually succeed at remaining politically neutral but their work is part of a policy process that has political implications.

There is, or should be, a difference between politics – meaning the risks and rewards of governing, and partisanship – meaning a more narrow advocacy of certain positions. In a highly partisan atmosphere, policy makers are more likely to question why intelligence officers raise questions about preferred policy choices, suspecting disloyalty as opposed to professional skepticism. This type of relationship can be more poisonous but there is little that intelligence officers can do within the proper bounds of their profession, to reverse this.

The early years of this century saw the appearance of several books that were written and published independently of one another but were related in terms of their subject matter: how people think and make assessments and judgments. In chronological order they were: *The Tipping Point* (2000); *The Wisdom of Crowds* (2004); *Blink* (2005); *The Black Swan* (2007); and *Thinking Fast and Slow* (2011). Each of these books has its supporters and critics. Are they helpful to intelligence analysis?

To take them in order:

- Malcolm Gladwell's *The Tipping Point* is about spotting that point where certain ideas or concepts in everyday life catch on and spread quickly: the tipping point. As a means of examining how something happened after the fact it may offer a useful framework but it offers little estimative or forward-looking promise. The Arab Spring would appear to be a classic example of the kind of movement that Gladwell discusses but the dynamics of the movement do not correspond to his major factors. Even after the fact, the Arab Spring remains somewhat difficult to understand.

- James Surowiecki's *The Wisdom of Crowds* argues that aggregating certain information in groups can result in better decisions than individuals could have made. Surowiecki says that this does not work all the time and cites counter-examples to his argument. There is some applicability to intelligence analysis as it is both an individual and group activity. That is, one individual analyst usually writes the first draft, after which it may be seen, reviewed, commented on, and even rewritten by one or several analysts. But experience in intelligence analysis argues that the greatest challenges in these group activities is not achieving wisdom but avoiding lowest common denominator decisions and group-think. The dynamics of the group is often the greatest threat to good analysis. Social media may also be one of the best examples of the flaws in the wisdom of crowds. A certain herd mentality can take over that has nothing to do with wisdom. For example, in the immediate aftermath of the 2013 Boston Marathon bombing, several social media users mis-identified a missing American student of Pakistani descent as one of the likely suspects. He was not, but social media and then some mainstream media picked up the story and kept repeating it.

- *Blink*, by Malcolm Gladwell again, discusses the concept that spontaneous decisions based on very limited information ("thin slicing") may be just as good as those that are fully considered. There is much to be said in favor of the gifted, intuitive analyst but they are not as plentiful as one might wish and it is not a skill that can be easily codified and then transmitted. As with all other professions, there are some intelligence analysts who simply are more gifted than their peers but we have not been able to find a way to replicate them intellectually. Moreover, even if an analyst has this gift, explaining it to a policy maker can be difficult unless the policy maker – or the analyst's superiors – has an underlying confidence in the analyst's inherent superior judgment. Without this confidence in hand, the analyst is unlikely to be seen as very convincing. There are times when the analytic manager or policy makers have to trust an analyst's "gut" but you first must have a very firm sense of how reliable and insightful that "gut" is.

The Intelligence Advanced Research Projects Activity (IARPA), an Intelligence Community office that invests in high-risk but potentially high-pay-off research has sponsored the Good Judgement Project, which seeks to identify the qualities that result in a "super forecaster." The single most important indicator is sheer talent, abetted by training, teaming, and aggregating forecasts. Superior native talent either exists or it does not. It is why some people are better than their peers in any human endeavor, they simply have more innate talent. This characteristic can be honed and shaped but it cannot be created.

- Nassim Nicholas Taleb's *The Black Swan* discusses events that come as a surprise but then are rationalized by hindsight. (It was an assumed verity among Europeans that black swans did not exist, until they were discovered in Australia.) The black swan concept goes to the idea of surprise, which is as inevitable in intelligence as it is in human affairs. Taleb understands that these events cannot often be forecast; his goal is to find ways to deal with the black swan events when they occur. This is useful although the intelligence community does not spend enough time on lessons learned and retrospection, largely because of the ongoing press of current and new issues that leaves little time and few resources to go back over past analyses.

- Daniel Kahneman's *Thinking Fast and Slow* is in some ways a refutation of *Blink*. Kahneman posits that there are two types of thinking: System 1 is quick, emotional, frequent, and subconscious, and corresponds to Gladwell's intuitive model; but System 2 is slow, logical, infrequent, and conscious. Kahneman says that, given the same input of information, the two types will arrive at different answers. It would be ideal to have both attributes in intelligence analysts but that would assume that everyone is "wired" the same way, which they are not. Instead, we have some analysts who are System 1 and some who are System 2. Having both types work together might be a preferred outcome, so long as one is wary of the intrusion of group dynamics, although this raises a question of how well the two types of thinkers can work together given their very different approaches to analysis. System 1 may be mere excitement but it is more subject to cognitive biases. System 2 thinking is less prone to these biases.

Some of this writing is almost akin to reading medieval tomes on alchemy. Instead of searching for the philosopher's stone that will be used to turn base metals into precious ones we are looking for the unique key or trait that will lead to better forecasts and less surprise. Certainly, we want analysts to be aware of how they think and what their strengths, weaknesses, and biases are. There should be an ongoing introspective aspect to good analysis. Two of my colleagues, Liza Krizan and David Moore, captured this in their very apt definition of critical thinking; "Thinking about how we are thinking while we are thinking." In other words, a good analyst should be assessing the quality of his or her work even as it is being done. This is not as difficult as it may sound but it does take some training, as the Good Judgment Project notes, and a good deal of honest self-awareness. These attributes may be more important than the various theories about how we think.

One of the largest challenges facing intelligence analysis is the ongoing flood of data that was discussed above.

From the point of view of an intelligence analyst a number of questions arises concerning the use of big data. The reader should understand that these various questions about the utility of big data are raised not as a means of downplaying the potential or importance of these data sets. Rather, these questions are raised because they will need to be answered before these data can be used consistently and successfully in the intelligence process.

The first question is its overall utility. Again, intelligence analysts cannot deal with and do not want or need all of the data on everything. Data in an undefined, unsorted mass is of little use. It has to be sorted and binned, and some data will get attention immediately, some later, and some not at all. This view reflects the view of some senior intelligence officials who are currently responsible for both data and its analysis. Two intelligence officials, one US and one allied, both said, "There has to be some front-end filtering." In other words, we cannot simply dump large amounts of data on analysts and hope for the best.

Who does this data filtering and on what basis? US intelligence collection has been guided by the National Intelligence Priorities Framework (NIPF), which reflects policy makers' priorities, as it should do. The NIPF establishes a hierarchy of relative importance among issues and also designates the appropriate types of collection for that issue. Under DNI Clapper, this system was buttressed by Unifying Intelligence Strategies that assess the degree to which collection and analysis are working in an integrated fashion and are achieving their intelligence goals for specific issues. If we use the NIPF as a guide to the use of data, how well will the priorities and the available data match? Or might we run the risk of denying ourselves potentially useful data because it does not appear to relate to a priority issue? For any of the issues discussed in the DNI's annual Worldwide Threat Assessment (Cyber and Technology; Terrorism; Weapons of Mass Destruction and Proliferation; Space and Counterspace; Counterintelligence; Transnational Organized Crime; Economics and Natural Resources; Human

Security) there are likely to be some useful data but these data will not be evenly distributed or of equal quality.

These rather basic questions may argue in favor of treating data as a separate intelligence stream. As noted above, data resemble both signals and measurement and signatures intelligence, and yet data are also different from both. Good analysts become familiar with the different types of collection and develop a sense for which types are more useful for the issues they must analyze. A similar process may be necessary for data. Despite what is bandied about, the analysts now being hired are not "digital natives." That phrase was coined by education expert Marc Prensky in 2001. Prensky said that today's students were "native speakers of the digital language of computers, video games, and the Internet." Part of Prensky's definition is accurate but most of these students and younger analysts are not digital natives if that term is meant to connote someone comfortably conversant with information technology and its major attributes and outcomes at a technical level. As Chris Inglis, a former Deputy Director of NSA, has pointed out, "They are not digital natives. They are apps users."

This is a crucial distinction because even the younger analysts do not necessarily think in the same terms as do information technologists. Currently, information technologists appear to be in the ascendant and some of them show little understanding or regard for how analysts work. When I pointed out to a senior intelligence technologist that the system he was building did not correspond to how analysts did their work, he seemed to be blithely unconcerned and said the analysts would have to change the way they worked.

Another important issue in dealing with big data is the choice of which algorithm or algorithms to use to begin the data analysis. There are many algorithms available and different algorithms can and likely will produce different results. How algorithms are chosen becomes a key issue in the ability to make use of the data. Besides having knowledgeable data scientists at work, there may be some examples from other types of intelligence that will prove to be useful.

First, as one specialist in the field noted, results of data analysis can be presented with confidence levels, just as other types of collection are presented. As the page "What We Mean When We Say" notes, a "low confidence" source may be seen as problematic but it may also be of use. Second, it may be necessary or even recommended to use more than one algorithm for data analysis, creating in effect, competitive analysis within the data set itself. But the possibility of varying outcomes depending on which algorithms are used will also raise questions about the overall reliability of the data, not in terms of it being corrupted but in terms of rather straightforward reliability based on outcomes. Many data experts who are also knowledgeable about intelligence might find either or both of the proposed solutions for dealing with variable outcomes to be acceptable but they do run counter to some of the more hyperbolic claims made about the utility of big data.

The ability of two distinct groups of professionals – data analysts and traditional analysts – being able to talk to one another with respect and understanding is also crucial. Without this not only will there be misunderstandings; there is the chance for outright hostility. I will use a non-intelligence example of the potential problem from the Cuban Missile Crisis in 1962. President John Kennedy ordered a quarantine of Cuba (rather than a blockade, which would have been an act of war in international law), which was established some 500 miles away from the Cuban coast. Secretary of Defense Robert McNamara went to the Flag Plot, the Navy's command center, as Soviet ships continued to sail towards Cuba and the quarantine line. McNamara asked Admiral George Anderson, the Chief of Naval Operations, with whom he did not have a good working relationship, what would happen if the Soviet ships crossed the quarantine line. Anderson picked up the Navy manual and said, "It's all here in the book." McNamara replied, "I don't care what John Paul Jones would have done. I want to know what you are going to do." Anderson invited the Secretary of Defense to leave the Flag Plot.

Therefore, some sort of intermediary may be necessary to deal with the data before it is passed to the analysts. Indeed, if the assumption that data may comprise its own collection stream is correct then we have to think about how we handle it. Just as there are single source analysts for the first stages of geospatial, signals and measurement and signature intelligence, and reports officers for human intelligence, we may need a similar construct for data. This then raises another question: Are all data the same in terms of attributes or how they are analyzed? Likely not. Just as different algorithms may produce different outcomes, different types of data will have to be analyzed in different ways and for different purposes in terms of their contribution to the intelligence process. Financial data, infrastructure data, internet of things data, social media data are all going to have different originating sources, provide somewhat different attributes and be analyzed in different ways. So it may not be sufficient to say, as one sometimes reads, "We need more data scientists." Which types? Just as the intelligence community does not hire scientists – it hires physicists, biologists, chemists, and so on – some specificity is likely necessary when hiring data analysts. Which ones are needed most, based on intelligence priorities and on which data sources seem most likely to yield useful intelligence?

What will these new data analysts produce and how will it be used? As with other collection streams, in some cases they may have fairly straightforward results: "We estimate that the GNP of Russia is about the same as Italy's." There is not much contention and it is easy to understand. But as we move into the vaguer area of correlation derived from data, issues of interpretation and preference will begin to arise. Just as various collectors may show a preference for the INT they work on, data analysts are likely to have more faith, at least on occasion, in what their data supposedly say than do some analysts. Or, just as people who process, exploit, and conduct "first tier" analysis of other types of collection are needed sometimes to explain to multi- or all-source analysts what they have found, the same will be true for data analysts. The key here is to make sure that this does not turn into a conversation of the deaf between the data analysts and what we might call the traditional analysts. It will also be incumbent upon these data analysts to show, to the degree that it is possible, that their data are both comprehensive and comprehensible. They will also have to be intellectually honest about weak points or uncertainties in their data analysis.

Assuming that we have somehow surmounted these various challenges, what is the analytic outcome? It is important to understand that senior intelligence officials and senior policy makers do not want data. I heard the senior intelligence officer at US Central Command say exactly that: "I don't want data; I want knowledge and expertise. I want an analyst in front of my desk who knows what he is talking about." In some cases the output of data may be knowledge; in other cases it will not, especially as we move into the more speculative aspects of correlation. Data analysts will presumably have expertise; they may not have knowledge. You cannot present large amounts of data to a senior official. They may not understand it and they are very likely going to ignore it. So, even if we devote the resources to more data analysis this will have to be "boiled down" or summarized in such a way that a policy maker can make sense of it and then make use of it. Will subtleties or contradictions among the data be lost in this process? How will this affect correlations drawn from the data, which may be speculative?

Second, policy makers want more than just what intelligence officers know. Colin Powell said on several occasions to his intelligence officers: "Tell me what you know; tell me what you don't know; and tell me what you think." Similarly, Donald Rumsfeld also wanted to be made aware of the "known unknowns" – in other words, not just what the analysts know but what they are aware they do not know. This is crucial as the unknowns may very well be the areas where surprise happens. Will these missing pieces be apparent to data analysts? How do you determine that you are missing data amidst a vast amount of data? If you can make that determination, then the proper course analytically is to give some thought to how your analysis would change if the unknowns became known, one way or the other. If there are unknowns in the data, will data analysts be willing to admit it? I raise this not because I question the professionalism of these people but I do have qualms when dealing with the more evangelical among them.

This data evangelism, if it may be called that, is potentially dangerous. Information technology and data provide opportunities, assuming that some sort of analysis is also involved, but they also create dependencies. Can the policy maker or the commander make a decision in the absence of data? Are soldiers being trained to make decisions in the absence of data? If not, they and we have a serious problem. The data may not be there. General William Sherman captured this notion very aptly when he compared the superior skills of his friend and colleague General Ulysses Grant to his own: "I'll tell you where [Grant] beats me though and where he beats the world. He doesn't give a damn about what the enemy does out of his sight, but it scares me like hell."

We actually teach intelligence analysts to perform analysis in the absence of abundant data. This, again, is where their knowledge and expertise come into play. Based upon what they know about the issue or situation up to date, where is it going next? The CIA sometimes refers to this as "analytic penetration," thinking your way through the problem despite the absence of newly collected intelligence. It is not easy and it is prone to error, as is all analysis, but sometimes it must be done. When I teach analysis I constantly emphasize the importance of telling the policy maker not only what you know, but what you do not know and what the uncertainties are. I believe it is crucial for the policy maker to comprehend and appreciate the extent of remaining uncertainties. Policy makers are going to make decisions based, to some extent, on the intelligence they receive. Even though one of the goals of intelligence analysis is to help the policy maker deal with uncertainties, this does not mean that remaining uncertainties should be ignored or masked. If anything, they should be highlighted. So, can this construct be an inherent part of data analytics?

One of the potential vectors to be aware of is what I call the "information technology Sukhomlinov effect." In military history there is a theory – stress, a theory – called the "Sukhomlinov effect": the side with the gaudier uniforms tends to lose. The effect is named after the Tsarist General Vladimir Sukhomlinov, who loved resplendent uniforms but whose military skills were lacking. In other words, large, complex information technology systems and floods of data will make it more difficult to craft useful analytic tools or to do useful analysis. There is a risk in creating systems that are so large and so complex that they end up being impediments rather than enablers. And yet, the siren song that ever more data that will produce more knowledge is alluring. In the mid-1990s, the concept of "dominant battlefield awareness" arose. Advocates held that with enough sensors and intelligence collection systems it should be possible to have "perfect knowledge" of a cube several hundred kilometers long, high, and deep behind the enemy's front line. However, one rarely has "perfect knowledge." There are often unknowns plus the fact that the enemy has a will of his own.

Carl von Clausewitz wrote about the "fog" of war and the concept of "friction," the small difficulties that accumulate and make it much more difficult to carry out one's plans. These concepts are as applicable to overall policy making as much as they are to warfare. There is always "fog," that is uncertainty, and there is always friction. One might argue that the more complex the system built to eliminate fog the more likely it is to produce more friction. Assuming that fog – either in war or in policy – cannot be entirely eliminated, is there a point of diminishing returns on investment in pursuing this data goal? Is there a point at which technology adds to the noise and friction but does not further eliminate the fog?

One of the goals of machine learning is autonomous machines – machines that can learn and then carry out certain tasks, perhaps better than can humans. Self-driving cars are an obvious but still very nascent example. Data advocates are excited by this development and hope to extend it to many fields. Will autonomy have a utility in national security policy?

It is difficult to imagine many national security decisions, at least at the macro level, where policy makers would be willing to allow a machine or machine generated data to make that decision for them, or to make a decision based solely on data. There are weapons systems that already have a certain degree of autonomy, including defensive systems determining incoming threats. But this is a far cry from either robotic warfare, which many view as destabilizing, or a machine that would make decisions about war and peace based solely on the data. The catastrophic doomsday machine in *Dr. Strangelove* quickly comes to mind although it should be noted that US physicists and nuclear strategists actually did examine the doomsday machine concept on a theoretical level in the 1950s. Simply put, it is extremely difficult to foresee circumstances in which policy makers would willingly cede control to computers or make decisions based solely on their output.

Rolling this back a step, it is also likely that most (but not all) policy makers are not going to give full confidence to intelligence analysis produced solely by data driven algorithms. First, as noted above, they are very unlikely to be either willing or able to work their way through great quantities of data. There is going to have be an intermediary or intermediaries. Someone is going to have to interpret and summarize what the data say or appear to say, with, one hopes, appropriate caveats about uncertainties and missing data. Policy makers are much more likely to take any such intelligence product and turn to an analyst to ask, "What do you think?" There is no substitute for the human in the loop, either in intelligence analysis or national security policy.

There is also a premium among senior officials on time management. They simply do not have the time to wade through long and dense presentations. During the Cold War, the US intelligence community produced an annual estimate on Soviet strategic forces. It comprised two very thick volumes and an executive summary that could run for as long as thirty pages. A former national security adviser once explained to me that he read the thirty-page executive summary and typed a two- or three-page summary for the President, along with some tabs where the President was urged to read the main text. This type of distillation is not unique. The question is whether data-driven analysis can be distilled and presented in a similar manner and still be useful to policy makers.

Increased use of data raises the issues of analytic tools. To be fair, we should distinguish between data analytic tools and those analytic tools that are not necessarily related to data. There are a great many tools in both categories and many suffer from a certain degree of hyperbole either by their creators or by satisfied customers. But the degree to which they are necessary is not similar.

Using data, making sense of it, trying to find patterns in it are all completely dependent on data analytic tools. You cannot hope to achieve the promised outcomes of using data without these tools. Each of the steps that are part of trying to make sense of raw collected data requires tools. Again, there is likely to be a gap between the data analysts using the tools and the outcomes as they are reported to policy makers. Just as policy makers do not want data, they do not care about which tools are used to analyze the data. They will be largely unaware of these tools, will have little sense of their strengths and weaknesses and would be hard put to choose among competing tools if asked. They will assume that the analysts know which tools to use when, and will do so, but it will be the very rare policy maker, now or in the immediate future, who will care about the tools used to analyze data. On the other hand, they may have ongoing concerns about the reliability of the data.

However, just as there has to be a means by which data analysts explain or translate their data for traditional analysts, there is likely to be some need to explain how the data were analyzed, if for no other reason than to give the non-data analysts an appropriate level of certainty when referring back to the analyzed data. This does not have to be a detailed explanation but it should be sufficient for the non-data analysts to have the same sense of certainty or uncertainty that they seek to convey to policy makers.

The other types of analytic tools can be employed to assist analysts in thinking through problems, sorting out available intelligence, thinking about how to present it, and so on. There are dozens of these tools as well and they largely fit into seven categories:

- Decomposition and visualization
- Idea generation
- Hypothesis generation and testing
- Scenarios and indicators
- Assessing cause and effect
- Challenge analysis
- Conflict management

However, the dependency noted between data analytics and tools does not exist between non-data analytics or traditional analytics and these other tools. Analysts can choose to use them or not, depending on their preferences or perceived needs. These tools can be useful but they are not mandatory.

The key issue with either set of tools is knowing which tool to use when. Not every tool is apt for every step in the data analytic process or useful for a given analytic problem. Therefore, to use the tools correctly, the analyst has to be familiar with the tools and know when to choose which tool. This may actually be easier for data analytics as there is a process with definable and distinct steps. This is not the case in the same formal sense for many of the issues dealt with by traditional analysts. There is also the tendency on the part of some analysts to become enamored of one or two tools and to use those even when they may not be the most appropriate. This is obviously problematic and underscores why analysts should familiarize themselves with a broader array of analytic tools. Psychologist Abraham Maslow put it succinctly, "When all you have is a hammer, everything looks like a nail."

The final issue to be considered is the future of the types of ways in which analysis is presented, which are usually referred to as products. This is something of a misnomer as it seems to connote an actual "production line," cranking out analysis, which is not quite the case. Still, it is the term used among analysts and analytic managers.

This is the one step in the overall intelligence process – dissemination – that has long been well handled. The issue in dissemination, which comes after the analysis has been completed, is: Which analytic vehicle (or product) should we use to get the right intelligence to the right policy maker at the right time and in the manner in which he or she prefers to see it? There is an established "product line," if you will, seven or eight types of analytic vehicles that can be selected. Some of these are standing or recurring formal types, such as the President's Daily Brief (PDB) or national intelligence estimates. Other types are more generic – briefings, memos – whose selection are driven by the criteria noted above, especially timeliness and required detail. It is also important to understand that the list is not restrictive or final in terms of choices. Analysts can go back and forth and use different analytic vehicles with the same policy maker over the course of an issue's development. For example, a crisis type of issue might first be handled

by a telephone call or a brief message, later followed up
with a more detailed paper or briefing, and so on. Again,
what matters is what intelligence is needed when and how.

The best way to have effective intelligence dissemination
is to talk with policy makers to determine what they need,
what they want (not the same as what they need), and how
they prefer to receive their intelligence. This outreach typically takes place with more senior appointees at the outset
of an administration. Middle- and lower-ranking policy
makers are not likely to get this personalized attention.
These officials will be more dependent on personal contacts
and relationships with intelligence officers. But these less
senior officials will often see the intelligence written for
their superiors rather than have intelligence written specifically for them.

Much has been made – perhaps too much – of the fact
that President Barack Obama received his morning briefing
on a tablet as opposed to a hard-copy binder, as had been
the case in the past. It is an interesting development but is
it a significant one, or are the enthusiasts confusing means
with ends?

There are some distinct advantages to presenting analysis
on a tablet or other similar device. The analyst or the reader
can easily access maps, photos, charts, or other supporting
material with links in the text. This has the useful visual
effect of reducing what might seem like an overwhelming
mass of material to a slim tablet. Also, the material can be
updated on the fly, as it were, as the briefer is en route to
the briefing. As useful as these attributes may be – and
much depends on the policy maker who is reading the
analysis – they do not change the substance of the analysis.
They may change the editing process. The analyst may
have more options as to what can be included, either up
front or as supporting material. The analyst also has to be
careful here to fight the temptation to lard up one's analysis
with as much supporting material as possible, which can
have a very distracting effect if not handled correctly. The
fact that much background or supporting material can be

appended does not mean that it should be appended. But the art of the analysis itself is not likely to have been effected. Moreover, at some point – regardless of the medium being used to present the analysis – updating has to stop; the writing and reviewing has to stop and the intelligence has to be given or sent to the policy maker. One of the concerns that analysts often have is that something important will occur after they have finalized their product and that the policy maker will be aware of this change even as he or she is reading the analysis for the first time and will think less of the analysis, or the analyst, for seeming to be unaware or behind the rush of events. In practical terms, there is not much that can be done about this. Again, at some point updating has to stop. One way in which this is dealt with is to put what is called an "ICOD," or intelligence cut-off date, at the top of the memo, showing the time and date at which the memo was finalized. This allows the policy maker to understand that the analysis at hand has a temporal end point and analysts cannot be held responsible within that paper for events that occurred after the ICOD. The use of the intelligence cut-off date is not terribly elegant but it is effective.

Still, the point remains that the means of delivering intelligence analysis, whether in hard copy or soft copy, via paper or a device, offer different choices in terms of presentation and back-up material but it does not – or should not – affect materially the core elements of crafting good analysis: something that is timely, well-written, easy to understand, and clear as to the knowns and the unknowns, and the certainties and uncertainties.

The premise of this chapter is that intelligence analysis will continue to be the main means of interaction between the intelligence officer and the policy maker. Equally important is the goal of achieving value-added analysis, which in turn requires both knowledge and expertise.

Just as intelligence agencies cannot collect against every target, so they cannot give each nation or each issue equal attention. That is the rationale for a priority system. Certain issues will remain high on the priorities list while others will, if the priorities system is managed both rigorously and honestly, move up and down on the list, presumably getting more or less attention as their position changes, reflecting change in the interests or priorities of policy makers. This also has implications for the value-added goal. Issues that move from a lower priority position to a higher one are going to be less likely to have as many analysts available at the outset who have the desired expertise. Expertise, after all, comes in large measure from "time on target." There is no way to make up for a shortfall of experienced analysts on a given issue without going outside the bounds of intelligence agencies, which, as we have noted, is viewed problematically by many intelligence agencies. There is also a potential hazard in keeping analysts on a given issue or country for too long. They may grow jaded and lose their ability to see clearly that something new and different is happening. I saw this to some extent among some of my colleagues responsible for Soviet issues in the 1980s. They understood that Gorbachev was in some ways different from his predecessors; some even succumbed to bouts of "Gorby-mania," as it was called, becoming uncritically enamored of Gorbachev and his every act and utterance. But they could not accept that the Soviet Union, which had been the centerpiece of their careers, might be coming to an end.

The current focus in many Western nations on terrorism as a leading issue, if not the leading issue, also has some longer term implications for the value-add goal and expertise issues. Terrorism is, in many respects, a tactical issue and not a strategic one. Our foe is relatively small groups or even lone wolves. This type of enemy does not lend itself to strategic analysis, especially given the regional diversity of the problem and regular shifts that have taken place within the Sunni terrorist world as groups have risen and faded to be replaced by other groups. Intelligence agencies struggle to determine the cause but must continue to deal with the symptoms.

This also means that far less attention has been paid to reborn strategic issues, primarily Russia under Vladimir Putin and the rise of China. Potentially threatening nation-state issues may seem familiar and even comfortable to intelligence agency seniors but that is less likely to be the reaction of their junior analysts. A thirty-year-old analyst has no working knowledge of the Cold War and is more likely to have spent most of his or her time on either counter-terrorism or counter-insurgency. The transition from those types of issues to strategic nation-state issues is difficult but increasingly necessary.

Here we can fault intelligence managers for chasing the obvious. To some extent this is what they must do. They must be responsive to the issues that are of greater importance or urgency to policy makers. Nor do they have the luxury of being able to hold back some analysts in reserve. The idea of a perfect distribution of analysts among issues is illusory. It does not happen and it will not happen – beyond the fact that it would be very difficult to describe. But for analysis to be successful in the future – I would argue that intelligence analysis is reasonably successful now, not in every case but by and large – more thought has to be given to what I call non-linear events. By that I mean events that are entirely within the realm of the possible but are held to be unlikely. The Arab Spring, again, is a good example. Policy makers do not have the time or the inclination to do this. But intelligence officers should constantly be asking themselves "What if?" questions. This can be either negative or positive turns of events. And if they do not have a good answer as to how they would respond to this event then they need to rethink who is working on what and where additional expertise might come from.

In a world that is not dominated by a single issue, the way it was during the Cold War, a major factor in success will be flexibility, the ability to shift priorities and analysts quickly, and to have external support when necessary. The CIA sometimes refers to this as "analytic agility." However, analysts are largely hired against current or near-term needs and not long-term needs that are not seen as pressing or urgent. Therefore, these are limits to analytic agility – the requisite expertise simply may not be on hand. The political vector here is clear. It is the set of analytic responses that will determine the outcome.

One final observation: analysts and analytic managers want access – meaning they want their analysis to reach policy makers and they want to be included in meetings where they can add value. There is no way by which they can force their access upon unwilling policy makers. If policy makers choose to ignore intelligence or to exclude them, that is the policy makers' choice. This is why the initial relationship between intelligence and the new Trump administration has been so unsettling for intelligence officers, a sense of disregard if not disdain.

4

Governance Vectors

Governance – meaning the creation of policies, monitoring their execution, the proper conduct of permitted activities, oversight of activities – is an issue and requirement for all government (and corporate) entities. Are things being done for the right reasons and carried out correctly? The importance of this question should be obvious. However, for intelligence, governance is also more difficult. The main issue is secrecy – not because it allows people to do things that they should not but because it creates limits as to who has insight into activities. At the same time, secrecy remains an inherent part of and requirement for large parts of what intelligence does. Even if the requirements for secrecy are changing, as was discussed above and will be reconsidered in this chapter, some portion of intelligence activities will remain secret. Secrecy may diminish but it will not disappear. But proper governance of intelligence is essential.

Good governance of intelligence is important in any state because of the power inherent in knowing things that others do not know or carrying out actions that will also be largely unknown. But good governance of intelligence is much more important in democracies. First, many aspects of intelligence run counter to concepts or values that are central to democracies:

- Secret agencies within ostensibly open governments;
- Secret budgets;
- Limited oversight by legislatures;
- Authority to intercept communications and to conduct other types of surveillance under certain conditions;
- Authority to conduct covert actions – that is, secretly intervening in the affairs of other states, when authorized by proper individuals.

Second, and closely related to this first set of issues, intelligence agencies function in democracies by permission – by the permission of elected officials in the executive and legislature and thus by the permission and acceptance of the public. Good governance therefore is a necessary means to assure these stakeholders and to safeguard their continued support.

How do we reconcile these various attributes and actions of intelligence with the values and norms of a democratic state? There will always be a segment of the population that argues that these cannot be reconciled and therefore intelligence must be tightly restricted if not abandoned. That is obviously not the view here. Despite advances in and appeals to international law, the international system remains one in which the nation state is the primary actor and nation states are allowed, within some limits, to act in their own self-interest. Intelligence falls into this realm of *raison d'état*, which can exist with some semblance of order and rules without descending into a Hobbesian nightmare.

What do we mean by governance when referring to intelligence? It can mean any or all of the following:

- Control: the certainty that intelligence agencies are under the firm control of the policy makers and will not become a threat or undertake actions that threaten policy or the policy makers.

- Responsiveness: that intelligence agencies will carry out their duties – collection, analysis, and operations – in the manner prescribed by policy makers, remembering our underlying point that intelligence must be subordinate to policy. This can be interpreted in various ways. Senator Dianne Feinstein, chair of the Senate Intelligence Committee, told DNI James Clapper that she wanted the intelligence community to be "more efficient." Clapper disagreed, saying that the goal was an intelligence community that was "more effective."
- Oversight: that policy makers will be able to have knowledge about what the intelligence agencies are doing and that intelligence agencies will cooperate in these efforts. Oversight can and should come from policy makers in the executive and, in democracies, from legislators as well.
- Public support: in democracies, at least, there should be some level of public acceptance of, if not outright support for, intelligence activities that are being conducted by people who have been elected to office or by their duly appointed designees.

The actual emphasis placed on governance across each of the points noted above waxes and wanes over time, driven in part by political issues. Thus, in the United States during the first twenty-seven years of the Cold War there was a broad, bipartisan consensus on the nature of the Soviet threat and the need to respond to that threat across a range of policies and actions, including intelligence. Intelligence was probably one of the least frequently debated or discussed aspects of the Cold War struggle.

It took a series of events to undermine the consensus, beginning with the growing opposition to the Vietnam War. This was then compounded, first, by the Watergate scandal, which involved some former CIA employees and, more fundamentally, eroded overall trust in government; and, second, by the leak of the "Family Jewels" report in late December 1974. This 698-page report of questionable activities conducted over the years by the CIA, which had been compiled at the order of Director of Central Intelligence James Schlesinger during Watergate, led to months of public investigations and revelations. These had two effects: creating a more vigorous oversight system in the Congress and making US intelligence fair game for revelations and leaks in a manner that had not been seen before. Intelligence had to learn to operate with greater scrutiny and occasional publicity. The earlier era of gentlemanly *laissez faire* by Congress and the press never returned.

Similarly, the emphasis on intelligence governance issues today is also driven by several issues, especially the long war against terrorists and the many operational questions this has raised, especially about various operations: renditions (extra-judicial arrests), prolonged incarceration, interrogation techniques, and the use of armed drones against terrorists who are often embedded in civilian populations. Then there is the legacy of the 2002 national intelligence estimate on Iraq's weapons of mass destruction programs and the widely held but erroneous view that this estimate is what caused the war. There is also the highly corrosive effect of massive leaks of sensitive intelligence, especially by Edward Snowden, far beyond the two collection programs that he claimed spurred his actions. Taken together, these various events have created a new debate over intelligence governance.

We should note an overall change in the security environment. During the Cold War, the sense of threat was real but was focused primarily on one nation state: the Soviet Union. Intelligence in this context was extremely secret, with some agencies not even being acknowledged as existing. The threat today is less overwhelming but more diverse and more hydra-like, requiring a change in how intelligence approaches its responsibilities. Sir David Omand, who served as the first Security and Intelligence Co-ordinator in the

British government, describes this as a transition from the secret state to the protecting state. These are very different functions, requiring differences in governance.

One final underlying point must be noted and stressed again: within democracies, intelligence is a service. Intelligence exists only to provide analytic and operational support to policy makers; intelligence has no independent existence. If intelligence activities cannot be related back to some policy requirement then they are simply out of bounds. But even when intelligence is performing properly as a service, several governance issues arise and will be important determinants of how intelligence functions in the years to come. The ultimate arbiter of these issues is not the intelligence agencies but the policy makers, who will – to greater or lesser degrees – also reflect their understanding of the views of their publics.

That said, we should also acknowledge that debates over intelligence policy take place largely among elites: national security experts from different parts of the political spectrum, civil liberties watchdogs, and some segments of the press – but not among the public at large. Rightly or wrongly, intelligence remains a remote and somewhat poorly understood function to the general public.

Although there have always been advocates for greater openness in intelligence, the use and advocacy of the term "transparency" is more recent, arising initially from concerns about the use of unmanned aerial vehicles (UAVs) or drones in the war against terrorists. The use of a UAV in 2011 to kill Anwar al-Awlaki, a US citizen hiding in Yemen who actively promoted attacks on the United States, and calls by critics of the drone program for an accounting of civilians killed in drone strikes were the two immediate factors giving rise to the call for greater transparency. The massive leak of collection programs (and much else) by Edward Snowden gave added emphasis to the transparency idea.

It should be noted that, in a legal memo released in June 2014, the US Department of Justice enumerated the limited conditions under which a US citizen could be killed as part of the campaign against terrorists, responding to the legal issues raised by the Fifth Amendment to the Constitution, which states, inter alia, that no person shall "be deprived of life, liberty, or property, without due process of law." In July 2016, the Obama administration released figures for civilians killed in drone strikes in areas other than Syria, Afghanistan, and Iraq. Needless to say, neither release satisfied critics of the drone program or US policy.

Calls for transparency are usually rooted in claims that "the public has a right to know." Although some aspects of public knowledge about what their government is doing is essential to democracy, this right varies from nation to nation in how it is stated and enforced. In some states it is written into their constitution. In the United States, a "right to know" is not among the enumerated rights in the Constitution and is very different from freedom of the press, which is in the First Amendment to the Constitution and safeguards the ability of the press to print whatever they want without interference or prior consent. Many nations, including the United States, have acts enabling individuals to have access to government information but many of these nations – including the United States and Britain – also create exemptions for certain types of national security information.

Thus, the core issue in transparency is: how much information about intelligence should be shared with the public and at what risk or cost? The Office of the Director of National Intelligence recognized both the positive aspects of transparency – greater public support – and the risks when issuing its *Principles of Transparency* in February 2015 and an implementation plan for these principles in October 2015. There are four guiding principles:

(1) Provide appropriate transparency to enhance public understanding of the Intelligence Community
(2) Be proactive and clear in making information publicly available

(3) Protect information about intelligence sources, methods, and activities

(4) Align IC roles, resources, processes, and policies to support transparency implementation.

The main goal of the program is very clearly stated, quoting President Barack Obama: "for our intelligence community to be effective over the long haul, we must maintain the trust of the American people, and people around the world – we will reform programs and procedures in place to provide greater transparency."

This is a rather remarkable document for any intelligence service to issue and has been met with mixed reactions: consternation on the part of some current and former intelligence officers; complaints that it does not go far enough by some transparency advocates; and cynicism by some critics of intelligence. However, it has also been seen as a very savvy effort to be somewhat more forthcoming where possible and to recognize that the political/public dynamic surrounding intelligence has changed.

Interestingly, the Office of the Director of National Intelligence (ODNI) has also created series of websites devoted to making public "factual information related to the lawful foreign surveillance" programs, including a catalog of released documents, as well as statistics on the number of orders and estimated number of affected targets under various titles of the Foreign Intelligence Surveillance Act.

How much does transparency or efforts to be more transparent matter? As was noted above, initial efforts at transparency were seen as being inadequate or were rejected as being questionable in the case of the drone casualties report. But this underscores one of the important facets of intelligence as a public policy issue that was noted above: this is largely a conversation or debate among elites. The public at large is rarely deeply engaged in debates over intelligence – except, perhaps after episodes like 9/11 or other large-scale terrorist attacks – as it usually is remote from their lives. Most people will have little or no contact with or connection to intelligence agencies or activities and certainly much less so than they do with the military. The reaction of the US public to the Snowden leaks is instructive: there was little reaction at all and little concern that the government was invading their privacy. Admittedly, reactions among the publics in Europe were different but they also tend to have differing views on intelligence and intelligence surveillance, especially that stemming from the United States. This is especially true in Germany, reflecting their twentieth-century experience of the Gestapo followed, in what became East Germany, by the Stasi. However, it is fair to assume that the transparency policy may also be envisioned as a potential antidote to leaks, which will be discussed below.

As noted, during the George W. Bush administration (2001–9) there was a period in which the key judgments of several national intelligence estimates were released, largely in response to pressure from political opponents of the administration. The declassified summaries became fodder in highly partisan debates and did little to advance the cause of transparency. Again, Director of National Intelligence Mike McConnell opposed further releases not only because of the partisan political effects but also because these were beginning to affect the quality of the analysis, as some analysts came to be concerned about having their work dragged into partisan (as opposed to policy) debates. Perhaps more telling about the perils of declassifying intelligence was the experience related to Iraqi weapons of mass destruction. Secretary of State Colin Powell laid out the US case for military action against Saddam Hussein in an appearance before the UN Security Council, citing the national intelligence estimate on Iraqi WMD and some of the underlying intelligence. Despite what seemed to be a strong case at the time, the Security Council did not vote to authorize military action against Iraq. For example, French Foreign Minister Dominique de Villepin did not question the need to disarm Iraq but preferred ongoing inspections before a recourse to war. So, first, the intelligence presented by Powell proved to be unconvincing, largely for political reasons. Second, it turned out that the estimate on Iraq WMD was incorrect, with tremendous consequences for the ongoing credibility of US, British, and Australian intelligence. It would not be correct to argue that making analysis transparent should be avoided as a means of safeguarding agencies' reputation. One has to be willing to stand on the quality of one's analysis. But there are risks, which may or may not be justified, in doing so in a public forum as opposed to discussing it with policy makers that have to be considered.

Allegations of Russian interference in the 2016 US election also show the limits of transparency in discussions about the Intelligence Community assessment released in January 2017. Although some faulted the report for not being explicit about the intelligence sources, others believed that a close reading of the report revealed a great deal about the sources. The report also offered a very detailed explanation of how US intelligence comes to analytic judgments. However, then-President-elect Trump and his supporters rejected the report, largely because they believed the report questioned the legitimacy of Trump's election, which it did not. Thus, transparency can be a mixed blessing. Moreover, as noted, intelligence is always part of the larger political and policy process, and will be judged not just by accuracy, objectivity, and transparency also by the political milieu.

Calls for transparency have also extended to operations, especially the use of drones, as noted above. It is not entirely clear why the drones, as opposed to other weapons, have prompted this debate. Concerns about civilian casualties are understandable but other weapons, specifically the use of manned bombers, would likely produce even more civilian casualties. The targeting of drones is not perfect – no weapon system is – but they are far more surgical and precise than most bomber-delivered munitions. The argument has also been made that drone strikes should be flown by the military and not the CIA – an argument with which CIA directors Michael Hayden and John Brennan would likely agree, as they both noted their desire to have fewer "targeteers" (as Hayden put it) and more analysts. But the Obama administration preferred to have a choice about who conducts drone strikes and was not willing to transfer this capacity entirely to the Defense Department. The final argument about drones, which goes directly to the issue of transparency, has been suggestions that a court should approve drone strikes just as the Foreign Intelligence Surveillance Court approves electronic surveillance. There is a large difference between intelligence collection and operations, which may be intelligence or military. In the United States, this would impinge on the President's role as commander-in-chief. What if the President disagreed and ordered a strike anyway? Moreover, the President is an elected official; federal judges are appointed. In summary, when it comes to operations calls for transparency quickly verge over into significant constitutional questions about roles and authority. More transparent information about certain operations is possible and may be beneficial but command and control transparency is highly unlikely to be achieved.

Transparency in intelligence programs certainly will continue and is likely to be an ongoing issue in terms of how much is made transparent. It is important, especially in democracies, for intelligence agencies to be seen as making an effort towards greater transparency where possible but these efforts are not likely to have much effect on those most strongly advocating more transparency.

The final issue to be considered in the future direction of transparency is the decisions about what is or is not to be shared in the future. These decisions will normally fall to the executive (unless the legislature can force the release of information via legislation), which also control the intelligence agencies. There will inevitably be accusations by the political opposition that the government is only making available that intelligence that supports its policies. There undoubtedly will be at least occasional temptations to do exactly that. Thus, for a policy of transparency to be politically successful, which is its ultimate aim, this policy will also have to be able to demonstrate a certain degree of political neutrality or the entire desired effect of transparency will be lost.

The discussion of transparency is very closely tied to the issue of secrecy. After all, if there was no secrecy then transparency would be much less of an issue.

In Chapter 2 secrecy was discussed in terms of collection. But there are many aspects of intelligence that include secrecy as an inherent attribute.

- Requirements: intelligence requirements, which, if done properly, are derived from policy makers' priorities, tend to be classified even though many of these priorities can be easily surmised or can be found in public documents, like the President's *National Security Strategy* or the Director of National Intelligence's annual *Worldwide Threat Assessment*. That said, insights into which issues or nations are higher or lower on the list can give insights into the likelihood of US collection efforts or the possibility of evading surveillance. Secrecy here is therefore tied to policy and to collection.
- Collection: the ability to collect needed intelligence without being impeded or deceived is a major reason for secrecy. Even though many aspects of collection are known in broad, or sometimes specific, terms most of collection falls within the US concept of "sources and methods," whose protection is a responsibility of the Director of National Intelligence.
- Analysis: the primary reason for classifying analysis is that it is derived from classified collection. But, over and above that concern, insights into what is being analyzed or what the analysis says can reveal information about priorities and requirements as well as the relative success of collection efforts, especially if analysis follows the preferred structure

of making clear what is known and what is unknown. Analysis can also reveal potential policy choices or initiatives.

- Operations: the need for secrecy in the planning and conduct of operations should be obvious, although there have been covert actions that were actually rather overt, debated openly by administrations and in Congress. The contemporaneous aid to the Mujahideen in Afghanistan and the Contras in Nicaragua during the Reagan administration are good examples, as are more recent efforts to arm Syrian groups opposed to the Bashar Assad regime.

There is a certain circular aspect to this requirement for secrecy, especially among requirements, collection, and analysis.

As noted earlier, there already has been a shift in the ratio of classified to unclassified collection since the end of the Cold War, going from eighty percent classified and twenty percent unclassified to the exact opposite ratios. Several advantages accrue from this shift, especially the ability to use the intelligence more widely beyond the confines of the government – with other states, with legislators, with the public. There are also risks, including the need to make an even stronger case for that now smaller part of intelligence collection that remains classified. At the same time, a wider use of intelligence, including analysis on such issues as epidemics and climate change can also be positive contributors to transparency, especially as some of the main actors on these issues will be non-governmental organizations and public interest groups.

Given the increased intelligence role that is expected for data and data analysis, a question arises: will those data and the resultant analysis be treated as "secret"? As noted earlier, much of the data being discussed, such as the internet of things or public utility or financial data or social media data, may be proprietary but they are not secret in the intelligence sense of the term. So, the first governance issue is how intelligence agencies will gain access to these data: request, court order, surreptitiously or through a trusted intermediary? Assuming we have resolved the access issue, which is a very large unknown at this point, we once again enter into a discussion of "the fact of" access versus the source. How the data will be obtained will play a role in this decision. Even if the data are given over by the data owners there may be concerns about others knowing about the request, similar to the discussion of requirements and collection above. However, given the recent discussions between the US government and mobile telephone manufacturers over the issue of encryption, it becomes less easy to see data owners freely giving over their data. How the data are analyzed will also be a factor. Will these be analytical tools and algorithms that are also proprietary or will they be owned by the intelligence agencies and therefore considered part of "sources and methods"?

Finally, it is highly probable that at least some portion of these data will involve "US persons," which in intelligence parlance means citizens, foreign nationals lawfully admitted for permanent residence or a business incorporated in the United States. In those cases, a court order would likely be necessary before intelligence agencies could access the data and there would also have to be "minimization procedures" to limit the scope of the data to only those individuals or entities who were legally deemed to be targets.

In short, before intelligence agencies enter the brave new world of big data analysis there are many significant governance issues that need to be settled.

Secrecy is an important attribute for intelligence but it is not a necessary attribute for all intelligence. There is much to be said for defaulting to open and unclassified intelligence as often as possible, if only to ease the use of intelligence and to minimize the political and security costs entailed in secret intelligence. The degree of secrecy will be closely related to decisions made about transparency. One of the problems to date has been the perception, largely accurate, that decisions made in favor of transparency and openness have largely come as reactions to events rather than as self-initiated ones. That said, there is certainly more openness and somewhat less secrecy in how US intelligence operates.

Assuming that the transparency policy is not reversed, which would entail significant political costs in its own regard, the key governance issue becomes defining the boundary line between transparent or unclassified information and that which remains secret. This line may not be rigid and may shift back and forth slightly over time but it is most likely that there will be a transparency point, perhaps not fully defined, beyond which national security officials are unwilling to go.

In democracies, at least, leaks are one of the unfortunate costs of government, not only for secret intelligence but for all sorts of closely held information. In the 1930s, President Franklin Roosevelt wondered why there were fewer leaks in Britain than in the United States, noting that "Britain has freedom of the press and tea parties." In the 1990s, Director of Central Intelligence George Tenet said the leak problem was worse than he had ever seen. The Obama administration (2009–17) was the most aggressive administration in US history in terms of the number of leak prosecutions, with nine cases brought to trial. People leak for a variety of reasons. Some of the main reasons are grievances or concerns about ongoing activities or programs, or simply to share information with someone as a means of displaying one's inside knowledge – showing off. Whistleblowers share the concern about ongoing activities or programs. The difference between the two is largely one of process. Several nations – including the United States, Britain, Australia – recognize the legitimacy of whistleblowing and have created procedures both to enable the act of legitimate whistleblowing and to protect whistleblowers from retaliation. Whistleblowers choose one path, leakers choose another. Either path is a difficult one to take but one has legal sanction and the other does not.

Leakers may argue that they have no other choice, that the legal protections for whistleblowers are flimsy or illusory. But many of those accused of leaking never tried the allowed path of whistleblowing, despite claims to having done so. For example, Edward Snowden, arguably the worst and most serious leaker in the history of US intelligence, claimed to have tried whistleblowing, but a unanimous bipartisan report by the House Intelligence Committee held that this was untrue, as were many of his other claims about his motives.

Concerns about leakers now largely fall under the term "insider threat." This can mean either someone who turns to espionage or someone who leaks, but the latter definition is currently the more prevalent one. Security agencies and businesses have invested increasing amounts of time and money in the problems of identifying and preventing losses via insider threat. It is very difficult to assess these programs in terms of utility or success: does the absence of leaks suggest that the program is a success or is it that no one intended to leak in the first place? Unless would-be leakers are caught in the act and then stopped before they can do damage there is no assured means of assessing the programs. Much attention is given to vetting programs during the hiring process, which is of some use but only if one has a very good sense of the profile or attributes of likely leakers. This is not dissimilar to the vetting conducted by intelligence agencies around the world, which is clearly an imperfect process at best given the recurrence of espionage. Very few recruits join any organization with the intent of doing harm from the outset. Rather, something happens during their career that creates a major turning point. As with counter-intelligence, one has to tread a very thin line between vigilance and paranoia – which can become a self-fulfilling prophecy in terms of employee behavior if carried too far.

I have suggested in other writings that one of the problems regarding insider threat is the effect of the relationship between individuals who customarily use social media and the online world. The desire, if not compulsion, to post endless photographs of oneself – even in the most mundane circumstances – and to share one's every thought and observation via social media can give one an exaggerated sense of self-importance. "I tweet, therefore I am." This may not have been the case for Edward Snowden but there remains something remarkable if not shocking for a thirty-year-old to believe that he has a clearer sense of the propriety and legality of certain intelligence programs than does the Congress and President of the United States. It is an act of astounding hubris.

The intelligence agencies recognize that avid social media users are the population among whom they will be recruiting for many years to come. Indeed, the person in this age cadre who does not use social media stands out as the odd case. Nor is it fair to suggest that all social media users suffer from over-inflated egos that will lead to leaking. The intelligence community had been grappling with the issue of whether or not they should look at applicants' social media posts. It is difficult to see why they would not. Many firms do so now as a matter of course. These do give the would-be employer some idea of the maturity and sense of propriety of the candidate. In March 2016, DNI James Clapper signed a new policy permitting the use of publicly available social media information as part of the security clearance process.

Is it possible to create a work environment in which the likelihood of insider threat is reduced? To some extent, probably. There will always be some employees who, for legitimate reasons or not, become malcontents. This is likely a statistical probability. But most people would likely prefer not to end up in such a category. It may be that some of the transparency initiatives discussed above will have the added benefit of suggesting to most employees that their voices can be heard and that there are legitimate ways in which to voice dissent. But another problem, at least in the United States, is the lack of universally applied standards regarding improper use of classified material. Several mid-level intelligence officials have been sent to jail for leaks but former CIA Director General David Petraeus was allowed to plead guilty to a misdemeanor (instead of a felony) and pay a fine, after sharing highly classified material with Paula Broadwell, with whom he was having an affair. Hillary Clinton's use of a private server for official State Department emails without any official punishment raises similar issues. Most recently, former Vice Chairman of the Joint Chiefs of Staff General James Cartwright pleaded guilty to lying to the FBI about his conversations with reporters about Iran's nuclear program. President Obama pardoned Cartwright in January 2017.

Finally, as noted above, the transparency policy may be seen as a potential means of limiting leaks, of assuring some who may be discontented that the government is doing all that is possible to operate with reasonable openness. This may work to some limited extent but it is doubtful that a robust transparency policy would have mattered to Bradley Manning, who was dealing with severe psychological issues, or Edward Snowden, whose inner vision is so much clearer than that of the people for whom he worked.

Another governance issue has already been referred to: relations between intelligence agencies and industry, especially telecommunications firms of all sorts. Two events have focused more attention on this relationship: revelations about the relationship between the National Security Agency and some of these firms and the FBI's efforts to get Apple to help break the encryption on the telephone owned by one of the San Bernardino terrorists. In several Western nations there has always been a close relationship between intelligence services and their respective industrial bases. The shift in attitudes on the part of industry seems to have come with the advent of the Internet and of firms that sell mobile telephones on a global basis.

There are at least two issues here. The first is the desire on the part of intelligence agencies to have someone (either the government or a firm) keep logs of the metadata – the fact of communications, date, time, location, duration – but not the actual communication itself, so that these can then be searched and linked to other devices or people if one of the two devices communicating can be tied to an illicit activity, such as terrorism. As noted, efforts to find a software alternative have not been successful. The second issue is the encryption that now is part of mobile telephones. These issues are not unique to the United States and have become part of the debate over countering terrorism in Britain and France as well. One of the issues is the limit on the expectation of privacy. If a person chooses to use a public means of communication, such as a telephone network – whether wired or wireless – or email, the "fact of" that use has little privacy protection. The firm providing the service knows of and logs the usage as the basis for its income. That information alone may be sufficient to look for links if there is a "reasonable suspicion" of a terrorism nexus. Within US practice, going to that second step – looking for links among the logged communications – can only be done under specific requirements overseen by the Justice Department and the courts.

Encryption is a thornier issue. Mobile telephones now come with very good "ubiquitous" (that is, end to end) encryption as well as the capacity to erase all data if repeated efforts are made to "guess" the passcode. The FBI argued that it only wanted to break the encryption on the phone in the San Bernardino case but Apple held that this would set a very bad precedent and would send a signal to foreign nations that it was acceptable to break into Apple phones, as if foreign services were waiting for US legal permission. Apple had helped the government in previous cases. The issue has divided technologists and also intelligence officers, some of whom – NSA Director Admiral Mike Rogers, former NSA Director and Director of National Intelligence Mike McConnell, and former Director of NSA and CIA Michael Hayden – side with industry on this issue and are in favor of strong encryption without "backdoors" allowing easier access. The arguments in favor of encryption include: more secure devices in an increasingly dangerous cyber environment, the possibility that other nations would make similar demands of these companies, and the danger that the "backdoor key" itself may not be entirely secure from compromise. Hayden has also argued that the metadata, which is more easily retrieved, should be sufficient in most cases to establish linkages.

One of the concerns of industries is the effect on their reputation and thus sales if they cooperate with government requests for access. On the other hand, if there was a terrorist attack that might have been prevented if certain information had been provided, there will be the same negative publicity result for the firm. The answer may be, ironically, to have a program structured like the 215 program, which focuses on metadata that can only be accessed on reasonable suspicion. But this still means that someone must collect and retain the records of the communications, either the provider or the government. And, if it is the provider, there has to be some agreed means by which those records can be queried.

We have not paid much attention yet to the issue of intelligence operations, often referred to as covert action. The definition of covert action in US law (50 US Code 3093 (e)) is helpful: "an activity or activities of the United States Government to influence political, economic, or military conditions abroad, where it is intended that the role of the United States Government will not be apparent or acknowledged publicly." In other words, one state is secretly interfering in some way in the internal affairs of another state for any number of policy reasons.

Covert action can be conducted by one state against another even though they are not formally at war. There are no agreed international rules about covert action and, given their nature, it is difficult to see how there could be. Few states acknowledge undertaking covert action, even though the United States has, somewhat ironically, defined covert action in a public law. The concept of "plausible deniability" is central to the conduct of covert action. There are, however, some unwritten rules about the conduct of intelligence activities. Those states that do allow assassination – the United States does not – tend to draw the line at other heads of state. Foreign nationals caught spying are not executed; they are jailed and are sometimes exchanged for other nationals. (Citizens caught spying against their own country have no such safeguards, either against execution or in the expectation that they will be traded.)

Legal definitions aside, covert action is sometimes thought of as "the third way," an option between diplomacy and the overt use of military force. These actions can be extremely risky. As DCI Richard Helms pointed out: "Espionage and covert action are where you get into trouble. They are, by definition, illegal in the country in which you are conducting them." The capability to conduct covert action therefore gives a fair amount of power and responsibility to that part of the intelligence apparatus. The same governance concerns with which we opened the chapter apply to covert action: control, legality, responsiveness, and the all-important issue of legal authorization. Obviously, the risks and concerns can be somewhat greater in covert action than they are in other aspects of intelligence. Also, covert action – perhaps more than any other intelligence activity with the possible exception of surveillance – is the single area where some people believe democratic states are violating their ideals.

Although some nations, such as Canada, eschew covert action (Canada also eschews espionage), many states find this a highly effective way to achieve certain preferred outcomes at lower risk and notice. Covert action can be disastrous, as in the failed Bay of Pigs invasion in 1961, or highly effective, as in the introduction of the Stuxnet virus into Iran's nuclear facility, causing destruction of several centrifuge cascades, which some analysts believe was an important step in moving Iran to accepting the nuclear agreement limiting their program for fifteen years.

For the United States, at least, covert action is an extremely personal issue for the President as only the President can order one. Different Presidents have shown different levels of acceptable risk, of possible violence or casualties in ordering or not ordering covert action. Covert action is also one area where there will be little willingness to be more transparent, although DCI William Colby, perhaps reflecting his tenure during prolonged congressional investigations of intelligence, observed, "You should assume that every covert action will become known eventually." This is not the case but it reflects the problem that some covert actions do leak and some also fail. Congress' ability to have greater insights into – and oversight of – covert action has been a recurring issue between the branches. Simply put, unless Congress specifically bans an activity – as it did in Nicaragua during the 1980s, or refuses to fund covert action capabilities – the President is free to conduct covert action.

As in so many other areas, the war on terrorism has refocused attention on covert action. Renditions, or extrajudicial arrest of terrorist suspects overseas, has been one area of debate. Beyond *raison d'état*, there is no international legal justification for renditions. There is also a disingenuous aspect to this issue as in most cases the government on whose soil the rendition takes place has some knowledge of it.

States that can and do conduct covert action are unlikely to abandon this capability if for no other reason than that policy makers find it attractive and useful. Therefore, the governance issues, especially regarding rules and oversight, become highly important.

Cyber – or, more properly, the use and misuse of cyber space – is one of those rare issues that transcends many boundaries in terms of use and threat. Although we have long been concerned about "dual use" activities, mostly in relation to weapons of mass destruction (such as the use of spent fuel rods from peaceful nuclear plants that contain small but usable amount of fissionable material), these nuclear, chemical, and biological materials or processes are not easily created by or accessible to anyone. With cyber space we have the opposite problem: this technology is both ubiquitous and accessible to virtually anyone. It is fair to say that most nations with capabilities to act in cyber space have likely done so: for reconnaissance, for collection or for operations. Given that the main or primary function of intelligence is warning of strategic surprise, cyber space attacks pose a particular problem. The history of the twentieth century is replete with strategic level surprise attacks: Japan's attack on the Russian fleet at Port Arthur in 1904; the German invasion of the Soviet Union in 1941; Pearl Harbor, also in 1941; Israel's pre-emptive air attacks in 1967; and the Egyptian–Syrian attacks in 1973 at the outset of the Yom Kippur War. Cyber space offers the ability to launch perhaps devastating attacks, presumably on infrastructure, with very few if any precursor indicators and at far less cost than amassing a military force. However, as DNI Clapper has pointed out, we are unlikely to see a "bolt from the blue" cyber attack, at least by nation states. All of the attacks noted above came after a period of deteriorating relations. Still, the ability to give warning about a strategic level cyber attack, especially by non-state actors, will pose a great challenge for intelligence services.

In some ways, cyber is the ideal tool for the conduct of covert action as one can be in contact with the target and yet still remote, and can plausibly deny being the culprit, given the difficulties of attribution over the Worldwide Web.

It is striking that the United States has twice in recent cases identified, to the degree possible, cyber space attackers. In the case of the cyber intrusions against the Democratic National Committee and a series of Wikileaks postings, DNI Clapper and the Department of Homeland Security issued the following statement in October 2016:

> The US Intelligence Community is confident that the Russian Government directed the recent compromises of emails from

US persons and institutions, including from US political organizations. The recent disclosures of alleged hacked emails…are consistent with the methods and motivations of Russian-directed efforts. These thefts and disclosures are intended to interfere with the US election process. Such activity is not new to Moscow – the Russians have used similar tactics and techniques across Europe and Eurasia, for example, to influence public opinion there. We believe, based on the scope and sensitivity of these efforts, that only Russia's most senior officials could have authorized these activities.

After the election, the January 2017 Intelligence Community Assessment included a consensus judgment (with varying degrees of confidence) among US intelligence agencies that Russia's aim was to affect the outcome of the election in favor of Donald Trump and that Vladimir Putin was cognizant of the activity. Russia, of course, denied the charge and asked for proof. In the case of the Dyn attack that made many popular websites (Twitter, Netflix, PayPal, et al.) inaccessible in October 2016, Clapper said this was likely the work of a non-state actor.

Is it possible to create rules on the use of cyber space? For the last several years many legal scholars have attempted to apply the rules of warfare (*jus ad bellum* – right to war; and *jus in bello* – right in war) to cyber space. These rules include necessity, proportionality, and the distinction between civilian and military targets. These efforts have not been successful to date in part because of the inability to agree on what cyber space and operations in cyber space mean. Cyber operations clearly can be used in conjunction with conventional military operations, but what about cyber operations as intelligence activities?

One solution might be doctrinal, meaning determining how and when cyber space will be used. For the United States, at least, this has proven to be something of a problem. Although there are reams of documents describing US cyber space policy, the issue of how cyber space will be used remains uncertain, beyond agreement that whatever a cyber activity is, whether military or intelligence, the President must authorize it. In many respects cyber space doctrine is, intellectually, where US atomic or nuclear weapons doctrine was in the years immediately following World War II. A series of books and reports written primarily by political scientists between 1946 and 1962 created US strategic nuclear doctrine. There are significant differences. Nuclear weapons and their launch systems (missiles, bombers, submarines) are tangible and can be tallied and tracked. Also, they are clearly weapons and have no other use. Moreover, the number of states with nuclear weapons has not expanded very much since 1945. There were, in 2016, nine states with this capability (US, Russia, Britain, France, China, India, Pakistan, North Korea, and Israel – although Israel neither confirms nor denies possession). Again, cyber is ubiquitous and has multiple legitimate uses.

But the important policy question once attribution for a cyber attack has been made with a sufficient degree of certainty is: now what? In January 1961, Fred Charles Iklé, then a political scientist and later the Under Secretary of Defense for Policy, wrote a seminal article in *Foreign Affairs*, entitled, "After Detection – What?" Iklé's article was about the possible policy options if violations of an arms control agreement were discovered but the issue is also pertinent to cyber space. If one has convincing intelligence about a cyber activity – then what? Calling out the perpetrator, as the US did with Russia, is one course but Russia has denied it, as would be expected. Then what? This appears to have been the US policy conundrum concerning Russian activity and the 2016 election. At this point, we have left the sphere of intelligence. Intelligence's role is to inform and to implement policy, not to create it. Cyber counter-moves or retaliation run the risk of an uncertain series of escalations. This concern does not rule them out but introduces a great deal of uncertainty that even good intelligence analysis may not be able to resolve.

In democracies, acts of war and certain intelligence activities are subject to debate between the executive and the legislature. Also, as we have seen, they can become part of the public discourse, as has been the case for the use of drones in the United States. Cyber space policy and the attendant intelligence requirements and potential actions would appear to be ripe for this discussion, much of which may take place in the hypothetical.

The oversight of intelligence agencies is important in all systems of government, if only for self-protection, but in democracies the issue goes deeper. Oversight, meaning "watchful and responsible care" or "regulatory supervision" is essential and central to all aspects of government. Are agencies and their employees doing what they are supposed to do? Are they being responsible with public funds? Are they operating within established legal limits? Oversight is a function of both the executive and legislative branches of any government, although they will tend to address the issue from their unique perspectives. For the executive leadership, whether a president or a prime minister, there is always some tension between the elected government, which is (a) partisan and (b) transient, versus the permanent bureaucracy, which sees itself as apolitical, permanent, and more expert in whatever the field is. Intelligence is part of this permanent bureaucracy. But the concept of service and of serving whoever wins the election is a sufficient initial bond at the outset of the relationship. The realm of fiction notwithstanding, there is no historical record to indicate that intelligence agencies in a democratic state have sought to weaken the incumbent government. There certainly have been periods of great tension between intelligence agencies and their political masters but not efforts by intelligence agencies to undermine or overthrow the government. Still, the executive wants to be assured of the effectiveness and propriety of intelligence activities and therefore must establish some liaison between the political leadership and the intelligence agencies.

This is not likely to change nor is the inherent inequality of the relationship likely to be adjusted. In brief, the relationship favors the elected political leaders, as it should.

It is their government and intelligence is just one of the many functions inherited as a result of electoral victory. And the so-called "Washington rule" about the relationship will also remain unchallenged, not only in the United States but in other democracies as well: "There are policy successes and intelligence failures but there are not policy failures and intelligence successes." One should also keep in mind that the more narrow professional benefits of success – as opposed to the larger issue of national security – are quite different for the two groups. For the political leadership it is re-election. For the intelligence agencies it is access to the political leaders, trust, and sufficient budgets.

It is in the oversight relationship between the legislature and the intelligence agencies that we are more likely to see some effect from the various change vectors we have been discussing. Even in a parliamentary system, where the Cabinet by definition controls a voting majority (and with exceptions for minority governments), the relationship between legislative overseers and the intelligence agencies is bound to be different. First, the agencies work for the prime minister or president and not the Parliament or Congress. Second, there is likely to be much more frequent and more intimate contact between the executive leadership and intelligence than is true for the legislators. Third, there will always be a substantial portion of the legislature made up of opposition politicians, who are free to question anything done by the executive, including its use of and relationship to intelligence.

A key issue in legislative oversight of intelligence is access to needed information. The issue of secrecy again argues for limits on what is said and to how many. On the other hand, it is extremely difficult to conduct effective oversight without access to at least some portion of this secret information. There is also the issue of the timeliness with which legislators receive this information. It has been stated repeatedly that the need for secrecy in intelligence collection has decreased and is likely to continue to do so. How might this affect intelligence oversight? It should mean that more intelligence can be shared without concern about leaks. But it also may lead some legislators to question the size of an intelligence budget that is increasingly dependent on open source intelligence. Greater use of unclassified intelligence also makes it easier for the opposition to use this same unclassified intelligence to call into question government policies or decisions.

Intelligence is either classified or it is not. Transparency, as we have seen, is not a decision based solely on classification but includes political goals as well. One of the goals of the transparency policy of US intelligence is to enhance public understanding of intelligence. The expectation is that this should lead to greater public support. Although it is not stated in the transparency goals, this greater public support should translate into greater support (or lessened criticism) from legislators, responding to the views of their constituents. But the executive will have, in many cases, a desire to limit the use of transparency when it comes to legislative oversight. The main issue will be the intelligence received by policy makers and the use to which it was put – or not – as well as the outcome of policy initiatives or intelligence operations. In cases where the policy is less than successful there is often the assumption on the part of opposition figures – perhaps genuine and perhaps not – that intelligence has been ignored. This may not be the case at all but critics either do not know or would prefer to ignore the role played by intelligence: it is neither oracular nor compulsory. An argument could be made that greater transparency would put a proper perspective on the role played by intelligence but it is more likely that this will not be an argument that many executive governments would find attractive. It is more likely that the executive would prefer to keep its relationship with intelligence agencies as private as possible. It is also likely that many executives would be concerned that once they embarked on a policy of greater transparency they could easily lose control of it and be forced to reveal ever increasing amounts of intelligence. So, the choice regarding transparency in oversight is, once again, how much transparency will be of benefit to engender support for intelligence and at what point should transparency be curtailed.

One of the more curious aspects of recent intelligence oversight in the United States has been the promulgation of analytic standards as part of the law creating the Director of National Intelligence. Although the report of the 9/11 Commission (formally, The National Commission on Terrorist Attacks Upon the United States) is widely seen as the main impetus for this legislation, the sections on analytic standards reflect more of the perceived shortcomings of intelligence with regard to Iraqi WMD. Section 1017 of the law sets out some broad requirements for the DNI with regard to analysis: encourage "sound analytic methods and tradecraft; ensure that analysis is based upon all sources available"; ensure that competitive analysis is conducted regularly; and "ensure that differences in analytic judgments are fully considered and brought to the attention of policymakers." These are all worthwhile goals but do they belong in legislation? And, having made these analytic goals laws, what is the penalty if they are not met?

Congress actually went beyond these standards and urged the new office of the DNI to come up with more detailed analytic standards. This task fell to the then-Deputy Assistant DNI for Analytic Integrity and Standards, Nancy Bernkopf Tucker. The standards produced by Tucker and her office were a good first cut, in some cases simply stating the obvious about how intelligence analysis should be crafted. But the reaction in Congress was totally unexpected. When Tucker briefed Congress on the new standards, she was asked how many analysts had been fired so far for failing to meet them.

I have written on several occasions on the need for reasonable standards for success or failure in intelligence analysis and have also pondered, along with my colleague Ronald Marks, what would be the effects of a determination that intelligence analysis may be as good as it will be – some analyses will be accurate, some will not but there is not likely to be a major improvement in the overall ratio. Why are the legislature's expectations for analysis seemingly more demanding? First, they are exposed to less intelligence analysis on a regular basis than is the executive branch, although the gap between the two has narrowed somewhat over the last several years, with more analysis going to Congress. Second, there is the issue of partisan politics. As noted, when the Bush administration bowed to political pressure and declassified the key judgments of national intelligence estimates on Iraq, these became ammunition in a highly partisan debate.

A final issue in legislative oversight of intelligence comes from the legislature's role in providing funding. Trying to determine a "return on investment" for intelligence spending is extremely difficult but important to the legislators who vote on budgets. What is the nation receiving in exchange for its intelligence expenditures? To use the United States as an example, in 2016, $71.8 billion was appropriated for intelligence. First, what does $71.8 billion worth of intelligence look like? How many collection platforms, how many analysts, how many written reports, how many operations? This is certainly not a useful or successful approach. Alternatively, can we assess intelligence based on outcomes? Did intelligence collect what the analysts and policy makers needed, when they needed it? Did intelligence provide the analysis that was needed and was it correct? For both collection and analysis, how often? In any of the major intelligence systems the answer will be "Yes" some of the time, but what is an acceptable ratio or percentage against the overall amount collected or number of analyses written? Were operations successes or failures? This is starker but operations are a much smaller part of intelligence than collection and analysis.

The search for efficiencies, a constant in government budgeting, is quite difficult when it comes to intelligence.

The disagreement on this point between Senator Feinstein and DNI Clapper has already been noted. Intelligence is not very efficient. In many ways it is like insurance – you can buy as much as you think you need, in large part in the hope or expectation of avoiding something catastrophic. But each satellite or drone can only collect so much in specific areas; analysts will be hard put to think faster or write faster. Clapper's "effectiveness" standard is a better one but still elusive.

Finally, given the major warning function of intelligence, can intelligence take credit for the things that did not happen? Perhaps. If it can be shown that intelligence thwarted an attack or positioned policy makers to make a successful move then intelligence has proved its worth, at least in those instances. Again, these will be a small number when compared to all of the decisions made over the course of a year. In the end, the answer to the budgetary return on investment question for intelligence may be somewhat impressionistic, which may be honest intellectually but is not successful politically.

The missing piece in legislative oversight is shared responsibility. Senator Arthur Vandenberg (R-Michigan), discussing foreign policy, said to President Harry Truman: "If you want us there for the landings, we have to be there for the take-offs." Legislatures play a key role in overall intelligence capability by dint of the fact that they pass a budget that determines the number of collection systems, the number of analysts, upgrading equipment, and soon. Unfortunately, when there is an "intelligence failure," a badly overused term, the legislatures disavow any responsibility. When Congress' Joint Inquiry, meaning the House and Senate Intelligence Committees, investigated 9/11, some members wanted to note that lower budgets in the 1990s passed by Congress might have been a factor in what happened. However, other members adamantly refused, placing all of the blame on the executive and especially on the intelligence agencies. This kind of behavior does little to support a more vigorous role for legislative overseers.

A final governance area to be considered is ethical and moral standards for intelligence. Some may find the concept odd if not implausible, that you can have such standards for an activity that seeks – in collection and in operations, at least – to violate norms of behavior that prevail in other circumstances. However, like any other profession, intelligence can and does have ethical and moral standards. Who establishes and enforces them? And for whose purpose are these written and publicized?

In 2014, DNI James Clapper unveiled a new *National Intelligence Strategy*, which included "Principles of Professional Ethics for the Intelligence Community." Clapper has said that work on these principles began in 2012 but the press of events delayed publication until 2014. In the interim, there had been Edward Snowden's leaks of NSA programs and much else, which again raised in some minds the propriety of US intelligence activities, and which also had some effect on the release of the principles, as Clapper admitted when releasing them. He also noted that the intended audience for these principles was not just the employees of the intelligence community but the public as well. The ethical principles are part of the broader transparency policy, and vice versa. This is perhaps best captured in the principle: "Stewardship: We are responsible stewards of the public trust;...and remain accountable to ourselves, our oversight institutions, and through those institutions, ultimately to the American people."

It is important, again, in a democracy to have such principles on the public record and to ensure that intelligence employees understand them. There is no magic formula to hiring or maintaining ethical employees. One has to hire good people and give them very clear boundaries as to what is allowed and what is not. But the system will always be imperfect. There is not a major governmental, religious or business enterprise that has not suffered from major ethical lapses by some employees.

Some people raise concerns that the fact of working in secret creates greater permission or license. There is no indication that this is the case and, again, the key is hiring good people and training them properly. But in the areas of human collection operations there is the problem that these same people may come into contact and work with very unsavory characters – drug dealers, terrorists, arms smugglers, human traffickers, and so on. Limitations or boundaries become more difficult if our goal is to penetrate these groups either to collect intelligence or, eventually, to act against them.

This became an issue for US intelligence in the mid-1990s. Without getting into too much detail, it became known that certain Guatemalan officers with whom the CIA had had relationships had committed human rights violations. The then-DCI, John Deutch, announced a new set of rules, requiring that any potential relationships with people suspected of having various criminal or human rights violations first required approval from CIA headquarters. But Deutch also gave official reprimands to some of the officers involved in Guatemala, which some saw as ex post facto justice. Rather strikingly, when Deutch announced the rules and the punishment at a CIA town hall, he was booed, an extremely unusual occurrence in any government agency. Deutch argued that he was giving the operators clear guidelines and that no recruitment was turned down as a result of the new rules. What was not known was how many recruitments were never attempted out of concern that these would have a negative effect on the officer's career. The Deutch rules were abandoned shortly after the 2001 terrorist attacks.

There are also probably limits on the degree to which one wants to specify which actions are banned or forbidden. In 1976, towards the end of the intelligence investigations in the United States, the Senate committee produced a complex legislative draft that included a list of banned activities. Former Secretary of Defense Clark Clifford, who was also one of the drafters of the 1947 National Security Act that created the CIA, argued that such a list was demeaning and implied things about possible past actions that were not true. Clifford also pointed out that anything not on the list could be deemed to be allowed, which was not the intention of the legislation's drafters. There are exceptions, of course. Beginning in 1976, successive US presidents (Gerald Ford, Jimmy Carter, Ronald Reagan) signed executive orders that included bans on assassinations, meaning either direct or indirect participation. (The Reagan order, E.O. 12333, December 1981, remains in effect.) However, the operations against Osama bin Laden and Anwar al-Awlaki, both in 2011, did not come under this ban as both men were categorized as enemy combatants actively engaged in operations against the United States, as opposed to political leaders.

The governance of intelligence is always difficult because of its peculiar attributes, especially secrecy and the nature of some of its activities. But effective governance is crucial both to a well-run intelligence community and to a democracy.

It is important to remember, again, that none of this takes place in the abstract. There is always a political context, or contexts. Internationally, is there a consensus on the nature of the threats the nation faces and, at least in broad terms, how to respond to that threat? As noted, there was a consensus about the Soviet threat and the conduct of the Cold War from its outset, in 1946 or 1947, until about 1975. After that, for the reasons cited above, some questioned the inimical nature of the Soviet Union and preferred to find ways to negotiate and be less confrontational. This devolved, in the United States and in Western Europe, into a partisan debate.

Terrorism has followed a somewhat similar arc, with great concern and solidarity in the period immediately following 9/11 and then a slow ebbing of that consensus as the conflict dragged on without any end in sight and as some of the actions taken against terrorists, or terrorist suspects, became known. Terrorism is also a much more emotional issue as it can affect people's daily lives whereas foreign threats always seem more remote.

Whether and how the Western allies respond to a revived and revanchist Russia can have a major effect on intelligence governance.

5
Looking Ahead

This final chapter has two purposes: to summarize from across the chapters the main potential vectors that have been identified; and to offer a glimpse or a suggestion of what may lie ahead for intelligence. The following are the major vectors of change that we have identified.

* Democratization of intelligence: many of the technologies (collection techniques, information technology) that were once the unilateral advantages of the intelligence services have become much more democratic. This is most obvious in the case of information technology, which can be found in most homes in the Western world, but it is also true for overhead imagery from space or the ability to access broad and diverse bodies of information rapidly and easily. This has several implications:
  ○ First, the intelligence playing field is more level. Certain nation states still possess far superior intelligence capabilities but many other states can play more fully, as can non-state actors, which may be the most important aspect of this leveling.

○ Second, this means that intelligence agencies, at least in democracies, have lost their monopoly in terms of controlling intelligence sources and in terms of being able to present these sources to policy makers. (In authoritarian states there are more restrictions on access to the Worldwide Web and other sources, which may allow them to control the flow of information but also limits their ability to take advantage of these other sources.) This introduces a notion of competition that did not exist before. Responded to properly, this competition should allow intelligence agencies to focus on those areas where they still have a unique advantage, thus managing their resources better, and also simply performing better in the face of this competition.

• Big Data: this remains an area where there is much promise but much remains uncertain. No one questions how much more data there are and there will be. Turning those data into a useful intelligence source is a different question.

○ First, there is the question of access: how will intelligence agencies get access to these data, much of which is proprietary? If the data are acquired clandestinely, how will that affect our ability to use these data, as they will then be classified in some way?

○ Second, these data will undoubtedly include a great deal of information about one's own nationals – either citizens or corporations. How will these data be segregated as per the legal requirements?

○ Not all data will be useful and not all data will be analyzed in the same manner. Hiring data scientists will not be enough. Specific types of data scientists will be needed, depending upon the data set.

○ It will be necessary to translate analyzed data into forms (mostly words) that can be accessed and understood by analysts and, most importantly, by policy makers. Data will be a contributor to intelligence but it will rarely be sufficient by itself. Few policy makers will be willing to make a decision based solely on data or data correlations.

○ There will also be the issue of algorithm choices. If different algorithms produce different results from the same data it may be necessary to analyze the data in several different ways and offer the results to analysts and to policy makers as alternative interpretations, perhaps with varying levels of confidence.

○ Reliability of the data will be an issue, especially when dealing with data coming from beyond the intelligence community. Have the data been influenced or manipulated in some way? How can you tell?

○ There are the interdependencies between the data and the various analytic tools and techniques that are essential to making sense of it, particularly artificial intelligence and machine learning.

○ Finally, at some point it may be worth considering making data, or DATA-INT, a separate collection stream so that it has the dedicated resources that it may require.

• Cyber Space: this is the most obvious area for both opportunity and vulnerability. Cyber offers means of collection, means to deceive collection, and means to conduct covert action. But each of these can be used by us or against us. Cyber, perhaps more than any other aspect of technology, exhibits the democratization discussed above, down to the level of the individual.

The debate about cyber appears to have shifted in the last months of 2016 from concerns about attribution, which is a major intelligence issue in cyber, to concerns about what to do after attribution has been made, which is a policy issue. In several of his past *Worldwide Threat Assessments*, Director of National Intelligence James Clapper had said that the cyber attribution problem was improving, without giving details, of course. The speed and certainty with which the Obama administration named Russia and Russian leaders as the source of political hacking in the 2016 US presidential election is striking. Russia, of course, denied this, in effect daring the United States to make public its intelligence, knowing this was highly unlikely if not dangerous. But once this attribution was made, there remained the question of what else to do, or what else could be done, beyond naming Russia as the perpetrator. To date, efforts to apply principles well understood from the nuclear rivalry of the Cold War – deterrence, escalation theory – have not been successful with cyber. (In December 2016, a senior cyber security expert at Kaspersky Lab, a Russian cyber security firm, and a Russian intelligence officer working in cyber were both arrested and charged with treason. Some assumed that their arrests related to the intelligence used by the United States in its election allegations. The arrests may also be related to entirely different matters and may even have been a means of sending a friendly signal to the new Trump administration.)

Finally, it may be worth considering making cyber a separate intelligence stream for much the same reasons as offered for data.

- Collection: along with the democratization noted above, there has been an increase in the availability of open sources, not only within open source itself but in the other collection disciplines as well. The most obvious one is geospatial intelligence, where commercial providers are now widely and easily available. But it may be true for human intelligence as well, mining social media for information about and insights into various human targets.

It would be an exaggeration to describe this as a general decline of secrecy. Intelligence will never be an entirely open enterprise. But a lessening in the reliance on secret sources has implications for intelligence. It should suggest a willingness at least to investigate other areas where open sources can be used. After all, these sources are less onerous to handle and offer increased opportunities for sharing – with allies, with legislatures, with the public. Ironically, the general mind set about intelligence – that it is about secrets – has the effect of giving less value to unclassified intelligence among those with whom it is shared. This open intelligence can sometimes be seen as a means of avoiding sharing the "good stuff." Still, the ability to rely more on open source and to focus classified collection on that intelligence which is truly secret should be seen as an opportunity, not a threat.

Finally, as data and cyber begin to provide more and more useful intelligence, assuming that the issues of collection and analysis can be solved, it may be both necessary and useful to think of them as separate intelligence streams, INTs in their own right. There is nothing sacred about the five intelligence types we now have. Any source as a working concept can be expanded as necessary.

- Analysis: When I first read Richard Helms' memoirs, *A Look over My Shoulder*, I was quite surprised to read: "the absolute essence of the intelligence profession rests in the production of current intelligence reports, memoranda, and National Estimates on which sound policy decisions can be made." After all, Helms' entire career, beginning in OSS, had been in operations until he became Deputy DCI, and then DCI. As an analyst, I was pleased but I was also surprised. People who knew Helms well confirmed that this had always been his view.

This is why the concept of "value-added" intelligence is so important. Good intelligence analysis has to be more than simply reporting what the sources say. Useful intelligence analysis offers context, meaning, assessment, and a range of possible outcomes, preferably ranked in order of likelihood. Policy makers can, of course, reject this value add if they disagree with it, arguing that it is simply the analyst's opinion. It is actually more than mere opinion; it is considered professional judgment. This may not make it correct but it should give the analysis weight and value.

Value add also becomes more important as more sources are not secret. The ability to add value is not dependent on the source but given the lessened cachet of open sources, this becomes more important for the future of intelligence analysis.

Analysis will remain the major interaction between intelligence and the policy makers, whether in written format or in briefings. How the intelligence is delivered, whether in hard copy or on some sort of tablet, is a question of means but does not affect the issue of substance. For intelligence officers, a key issue in providing analysis is managing expectations in terms of analysts' ability to be correct more often than not. This depends on the strength of one's intelligence sources; the analyst's ability and the time allowed to produce the analysis; the fact that – as National Intelligence Chairman Gregory Treverton often notes – intelligence is in the business of uncovering secrets, not mysteries; and the fact that we are writing about human beings, who can be changeable, unpredictable and, by our own lights, irrational. No one expects intelligence to be correct all of the time but no one can or will define where it might be allowed to be wrong on occasion.

Finally, analysis takes place and is offered up within a political milieu. Henry Kissinger once observed that academic arguments were so vicious because the stakes were so small. Policy making and intelligence analysis are not an academic seminar and there are many things that are at stake beyond the success of policy and correct analysis: agendas, careers, reputations. One of the great concerns of all intelligence managers and analysts is politicization, the forcing of conclusions in analysis to fit a political agenda. My experience suggests that the concern is greater than the reality, which is good, but the quality and purpose of intelligence will always be questioned by those who suspect some political agenda lying behind it – largely because they do not agree with the intelligence analysis or find that it is not supportive of their preferred policies or positions. These concerns and occasional accusations become more frequent in debates between the executive and the legislature.

• Governance: Again, effective oversight of all government activities is central to a democracy. The issues and strains in overseeing intelligence are different because of secrecy, because of the limited number of legislators who actually take part in or have a real feel for intelligence and intelligence oversight, and because there is a very limited public constituency that is truly interested in the issue.

The publication of standards for transparency and for ethical conduct are positive in and of themselves but they are also political documents, designed, in part, to increase public and legislative support and perhaps to stem leaking. This may reflect the nature of the main intelligence concern for the past fifteen years, terrorism, which is, fortunately, less threatening and less overwhelming than a nuclear armed Soviet Union but is combatted in a changed milieu of the twenty-four-hour news cycle and social media. Combatting non-state actors is, in some respects, much more difficult than confronting a hostile nation state. Former Secretary of State Lawrence Eagleburger said it was wrong to be nostalgic about the Cold War but it was a more straightforward issue with which to deal.

What seems to have been lost in debates over and criticism of US policy *vis-à-vis* terrorists is that this war was not, like Iraq, a "war of choice." Al Qaeda attacked the United States. One may question tactical choices in combatting terrorism but the United States had little choice but to respond vigorously.

Finally, governance and oversight also take place in a partisan political atmosphere. This creates friction of its own that cannot be easily separated from the more substantive issues about intelligence.

Looking Ahead

A frequent criticism of the intelligence community is that it is an industrial age process in an information highway era. Is this valid?

There is an established process for intelligence analysis:

- Requirements: what do the policy makers need to know, in what priority order and how quickly?
- Collection: what information do we need to respond to the policy makers' needs?
- Processing and exploitation: converting the raw collected intelligence into something analysts can use.
- Analysis: making sense of the collected intelligence, adding value whenever possible.
- Dissemination: choosing the right vehicle (paper, briefing, etc.) to get the analysis to the policy maker when they need it in the form they prefer.

- Consumption: the policy maker takes in the intelligence.
- Feedback: on rare occasions, the policy maker provides feedback.

The process is not unique to the United States. As I often explain when training analysts, the steps in the process make sense and the process works. I am not sure I would describe this as an industrial age process but it is most certainly an intellectual process and not a mechanical one. However, each iteration of the process is only as good as the weakest step and one can do each step in process correctly and still not arrive at the correct analytical answer.

If we were to try to modernize and update the process, which steps could be omitted or streamlined? That is very difficult to describe. Much has been accomplished over the decades to create efficiencies where possible. Word search programs and machine translation can help perform at least triage with signals intelligence. Analysts receive their intelligence in soft copy now, versus hard copy, and it is relatively easy to manage their incoming queue so they receive only the intelligence they need. Networking and various collaborative tools make it easier for analysts from across the intelligence community to work together. But the long pole in the tent of the intelligence process remains the intelligence analyst. Analysts can only read so fast and think so fast and write so fast, and they cannot respond to urgings to do any of these faster. If anything, continuing growth in the amount of intelligence that is collected and passed along to analysts will slow the system further. One answer might be to hire more analysts but that runs into budgetary issues for both the executive and the legislature. Alternatively, one can turn to intellectual triage, moving more analysts from less important or more quiescent issues to those that are more important or more urgent. Having been responsible for advising on such choices at a national level for three years, I can state that this works – up to a point. Inevitably, an issue arises that was either not receiving much attention or was wholly unforeseen – such as the Arab Spring – and then resource choices have to be reallocated on the fly.

Another critique of intelligence is that it is a bureaucratic structure fighting against networks, meaning terrorists primarily. Some critics argue that you have to be a network to defeat a network, the underlying concept being that networks have an inherent flexibility that large governmental structures do not. But their goals and means of operating are not the same. Is it necessary to ape your enemy to defeat him? A better question might be: Which aspects of my foe's structure and methodology might I profitably copy and which do not work for me at all? Flexibility is an admirable quality but within any intelligence enterprise there will be a need for some expertise by function (collection, analysis, operations, etc.). Everyone cannot do everyone else's job. As noted, the CIA for years has promoted the concept of "analytic agility," meaning the ability to move analysts from one area to another as needed. As we will discuss below, this can be done – up to a point. Each analyst has specific strengths that he or she can bring to various issues but there will also be issues where specific analysts have less to contribute.

Structurally, the US intelligence community is made up of "stovepipes," that is verticals built either around an INT or based on which policy maker is an agency's principal client. These verticals can be inhibitors to collaboration – or intelligence integration as DNI Clapper calls it. Are there alternative structures? Obviously, there could be but one also has to take into account that some organization has to be responsible for each INT – for managing collection systems, adjudicating priorities, processing, and exploiting the collected intelligence and disseminating it to the analysts who need it. Each INT is managed, collected, and processed somewhat differently, or vastly differently from the others. One could create a single collection entity but within it there would still be some sort of stovepipe array INT by INT.

The INT stovepipes are not inherently bad as long as they do not create impediments. We have discussed the problem of "collection ownership" which has been overcome to some extent with the cultural shift to "responsibility to provide." Integrating collectors to work towards more common goals is a constant work in progress but there has been significant progress under DNI Clapper's relentless emphasis on intelligence integration.

There is a second set of verticals for US intelligence. US intelligence is structured so that each senior policy maker has his or her own close-in, dedicated intelligence support. The President has CIA; the Secretary of State has the Bureau of intelligence and Research; the Secretary of Defense and the Chairman of the Joint Chiefs of Staff have the Defense Intelligence Agency; the Attorney General has the Federal Bureau of Investigation; the Secretary of Homeland Security has the Office of Intelligence and Analysis. There are alternative structures. The British government is served by the Joint Intelligence Committee, which is part of the Cabinet Office. But Britain has Cabinet government, which is different from a presidential system with department heads. Moreover, US Cabinet-level officials are highly unlikely to be willing to give up their own dedicated intelligence support.

As frequent as this sort of debate is among those knowledgeable about intelligence, is it the correct question? As noted above, and seconding DNI Clapper's exchange with Senator Dianne Feinstein, there is not very much that can be done to make intelligence efficient. Efficiency is not even the correct goal. The hallmark should be effectiveness, or improved effectiveness, which for intelligence can be summed up in the three main categories we have been discussing:

- Collection: Can we collect all that we need quickly enough and process and exploit the collected intelligence in a timely manner to get it to analysts or policy makers? Note the inclusion of processing and exploitation as a necessary part of this issue. The collected image, signal or even open source that is not processed and exploited is identical to the intelligence that was never collected. It has no value. Is there capacity within the system to collect and handle more intelligence? Do we want to make the investments necessary to do that? How will the growth in cyber and especially in data affect the collection system? Again, do we have the resources needed to exploit these new streams fully and in a timely manner?

- Analysis: No amount of technology can replace a knowledgeable analyst. As noted above, there are some technologies that can assist in certain aspects of analysis but the analyst remains central. If this is so, more and better attention should be given to how we both train and educate analysts and how we expect to see their careers develop over time. A robust lessons learned capacity would also be a great improvement.

One of the most difficult aspects in selecting analysts is determining which fields and types of expertise will be needed. Issues come and go, even very large and seemingly permanent issues, like the Soviet Union. This brings us back to the issue of analytic flexibility or agility. It is not possible to have analytic reserve that can be thrown into a sudden crisis. Every analyst is engaged every day in his or her area of responsibility. It is a zero-sum game. If more analysts need to work on the Arab Spring, for example, they have to come from somewhere, they have to be taken off other accounts. The analytic system understandably is dominated by the here and now issues. For years the predominant issue was the Soviet Union, although this had many different aspects: strategic forces; conventional forces; diplomacy; economics; internal politics and cohesion and so on. Since 2001, terrorism has been the dominant issue, although not to the same extent as was the Soviet Union. But we have ended up with a cadre of analysts, mostly hired after 9/11, who have little or no expertise or familiarity with strategic intelligence issues of the sort that were the mainstay of the Cold War and that now seem important again with the rise of China and a revanchist Russia.

Some thought can be given to training some analysts for the issues that are not at the top of the agenda or priority list but this is difficult to do for at least two reasons. First, analytic managers are too often loath to release analysts for training, especially if it appears to bear no relationship to their current tasks. Second, there is no guarantee that the correct issues will be chosen for this future-looking training.

Finally, assuming that the collection and algorithm issues for data are resolved to some extent, how will this intelligence stream, or streams be integrated into broader analysis so that the analysts can make use of it and can pass it along to policy makers in a way that they are most likely to understand it? Again, policy makers do not want and cannot use large amounts of data; they want the end results of data analysis, which may have to be presented with caveats or ranges of confidence.

- Operations: Gauging the effectiveness of operations has always been a bit more difficult than it appears. At a very simplistic level, an operation either succeeds for an acceptable cost or it does not. But there are also the long-term consequences and unintended consequences that can be considered as well. To use two well-known examples:
  - In 1953, the US government helped overthrow the government of Mohammed Mossadegh in Iran, bringing back the Shah. In 1979, the Shah fell from power to be replaced by the current theocracy, which continues to cite the United States

as the "Great Satan." This earlier intervention remains one of several stumbling blocks in US–Iranian relations.

○ After the Soviet invasion of Afghanistan, the United States provided largely overt covert assistance to the Mujaheddin. The Red Army was defeated in Afghanistan, which helped contribute to the collapse of the Soviet Union. The Mujaheddin morphed into the Taliban, a problem in and of itself, and a supporter of al Qaeda.

○ Therefore, were these operations successes or not? I have argued in other writings that these were successes in terms of their immediate goals and, also, that one cannot hope to foresee all of the long-range consequences. Some will disagree and I understand their position.

Operations are one aspect of intelligence that have been greatly affected by leaks, along with collection. The restraint that journalists once applied to some reporting about intelligence hardly exists any longer. It is difficult in the extreme to conduct successful operations or clandestine collection if they are subject to exposure.

Much of the future of intelligence will be determined not by what happens in intelligence but what happens in international politics. If intelligence undertakes its function properly, subordinated to policy, then intelligence will inevitably be affected by politics and policies. US intelligence was not created after World War II specifically to fight the Cold War (most of the other major national intelligence services predate the Cold War in some shape or form). But the Cold War helped determine forms and functions that continue to define US intelligence decades after the Cold War ended successfully. Similarly, the long war against terrorists has also shaped or re-shaped intelligence, fostering new types of collection, such as drones; new types of analysis, such as patterns of life; and operations that have, for some, skirted the lines of what is or is not acceptable. But the most profound change has been, in my view, going from a global strategic threat (the Soviet Union) to a series of possibly interconnected small group threats, meaning terrorists. At some level this is less national intelligence than it is police work. However, as noted, it is also a threat that publics feel and fear more directly than they did the seemingly more remote possibility of a super power nuclear exchange.

The intellectual transition from World War II to the Cold War was fairly seamless, facing one totalitarian state threat after having defeated the earlier one – albeit now with the added problem of nuclear weapons and then the capability to deliver them by intercontinental missiles. The end of the Cold War was rather abrupt, leaving US national security policy, at least, somewhat adrift. The terrorist attacks ten years later offered some clarity but not, as noted, in the same way that the Soviet Union had. Nation state issues can never leave the agenda entirely but they seemed less important or less urgent in most cases in the years following the end of the Cold War. If, as some suppose, nation state issues are now resurgent, then intelligence agencies will have to adjust again. The issues may look and feel familiar to long-time policy and intelligence veterans but they will be largely new to most of the intelligence agencies' employees.

What is strikingly different about the emerging nation state competition with China and with Russia is the near absence of any ideological content. Vladimir Putin may argue that Western values are corrupt and that there is something pure about long-time Russian values and traditions but this has little or no appeal beyond the borders of Russia. Similarly, China is ostensibly still a communist state, or at least one that is ruled by a Communist Party elite, but China does not – in fact it cannot – proselytize the advantages of a Marxist–Leninist–Maoist approach to economics and politics having largely abandoned any pretense to being such a state.

In the absence of ideology, the levers of power matter much more: internal cohesion, a stable political succession system, economics, resources, demography, allies, military capabilities. Most of these levers would argue against the long-term prospects for either Russia or China. This is where "linear thinking" by policy makers and especially by analysts becomes dangerous – assuming that the future is simply an extension of the present. Good intelligence officers always ask "What if?" questions: What might I expect to see if there was some major change – either positive or negative – in this situation? These changes may not come about but the intelligence agencies should be alert to the possibilities and looking for the signs of change.

The major change of the current and near-term period may not be a renewed nation state competition but the rise of non-state actors who are able to use cyber space for a variety of causes or goals – not just terrorists or criminals but hackers. Some have political or criminal agendas but some appear to operate largely to prove that they can. The Internet and Worldwide Web, as currently configured, gives them – or anyone else – tremendous reach and the ability to create mass disruption with little warning and perhaps no means of deterrence or even retaliation. This is not just a technical problem but also a doctrinal one that the United States does not appear to have solved as yet. Intelligence has an important role to play but it cannot, and should not, make policy decisions.

I always thought that being an intelligence officer was a privilege – not because I was privy to secrets but because I was given a unique opportunity to contribute to policy in furtherance of my nation's security. So long as intelligence services can continue to attract good people who will dedicate themselves to their profession that part of the future of intelligence, at least, will still be bright.

Further Reading

John Arquilla and David Ronfeldt, *In Athena's Camp: Preparing for Conflict in the Information Age.* Rand Corporation, 1997.

Richard Betts, *Enemies of Intelligence: Knowledge in Power in American National Security.* Columbia University Press, 2009.

Aaron Franklin Brantly, *The Decision to Attack: Military and Intelligence Cyber Decision-Making.* University of Georgia Press, 2016.

Timothy Chou, *Precision: Principles, Practices and Solutions for the Internet of Things.* lulu.com, 2016.

Jeffrey Cooper, *Curing Analytic Pathologies: Pathways to Improved Intelligence Analysis,* Center for the Study of Intelligence, Central Intelligence Agency, December 2005. https://www.cia.gov/library/center-for-the-study-of-intelligence/csi-publications/books-and-monographs/curing-analytic-pathologies-pathways-to-improved-intelligence-analysis-1/analytic_pathologies_report.pdf

J. Richard Hackman, *Collaborative Intelligence: Using Teams to Solve Hard Problems.* Berrett-Koehler Publishers, 2011.

Richards J. Heuer, Jr., *Psychology of Intelligence Analysis,* 2nd edn. Pherson Associates, 2007.

Robert Jervis, *Why Intelligence Fails: Lessons from the Iranian Revolution and the Iraq War.* Cornell University Press, 2011.

John D. Kelleher, Brian MacNamee, and Aoife D'Arcy, *Fundamentals of Machine Learning for Predictive Data Analytics: Algorithms, Worked Examples, and Case Studies.* The MIT Press, 2015.

David Omand, *Securing the State.* Oxford University Press, 2014.

Index